THE PARTNER'S

20 minute guide

A guide for partners about how to help their loved one change their substance use

cmc
center for motivation & change

THE PARTNER'S
20 minute guide

A guide for partners about how to help their loved one change their substance use

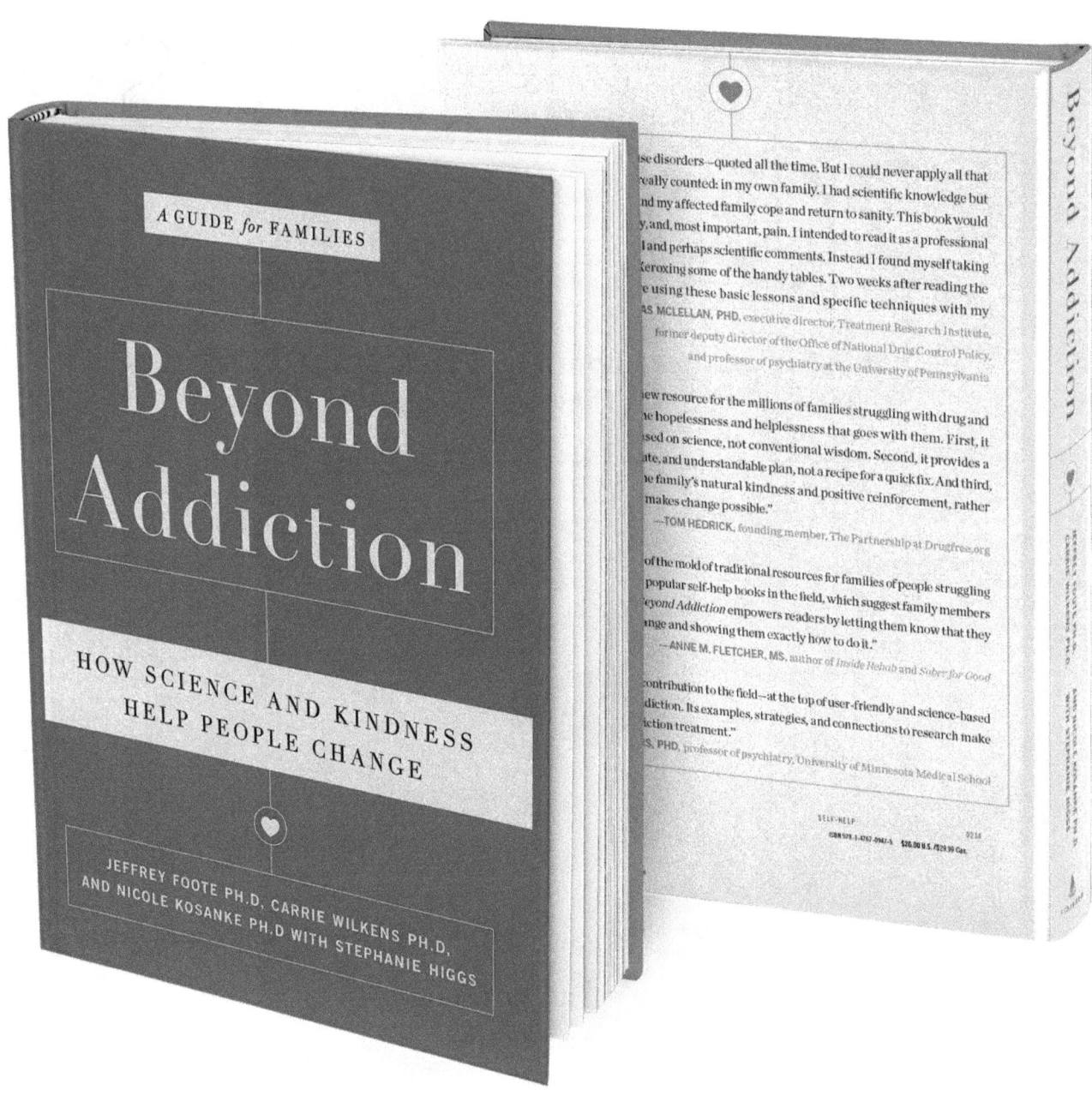

Additional CMC Resource: <u>Beyond Addiction</u> offers a groundbreaking, science-based guide to helping loved ones overcome addiction problems and compulsive behaviors.

Available on Amazon.com, BN.com, and at a bookstore near you.
For more information, visit http://beyondaddictionbook.com.

THE PARTNER'S 20 MINUTE GUIDE
SECOND EDITION

A guide for partners about how to help their loved one change their substance use

cmc center for motivation & change

2016

First Printing: 2014

Second Edition

ISBN 978-1-329-80710-5

Center for Motivation & Change

276 Fifth Avenue Suite 1101

New York, NY 10001

www.motivationandchange.com

Ordering Information:

Special discounts are available on quantity purchases by placing your order on Lulu.com. Please visit http://the20minuteguide.com/cmc/purchase-partners-20-minute-guide for details.

U.S. trade bookstores and wholesalers: This book may be purchased and stocked through Ingram. See http://www.ingramcontent.com/ for more details.

CONTENTS

CHAPTER I

INTRODUCTION

1. WELCOME TO THE PARTNER'S 20 MINUTE GUIDE

Being in a committed or long-term relationship can be hard during the best of times. If one member of the partnership has a substance use problem, it can be extremely difficult and may even feel impossible. If you are reading this, you are likely a very concerned partner* who is looking for guidance about how to help your loved one who is using substances (or engaging in other risky behaviors). You may have mild concerns about his/her focus at work, choice of friends, withdrawn or negative communication with you, or you may be facing terrifying problems that have the potential to negatively affect your entire family. Whatever your particular mix of worries about your relationship, the problems that come along with your partner's use of substances can be nerve-racking—sometimes explosive.

> *A note to girl/boyfriends, wives and husbands, hetero and homosexual partners, married and not: please understand "partner" as shorthand and feel welcome here.

A COMPLEX PROBLEM FOR YOUR PARTNER

The social, psychological, and biological factors that play into the decision to use substances are complex. Many people who develop problems with substances also struggle with psychiatric problems like depression, bipolar disorder, anxiety problems, and ADHD. They may also be contending with problems involving employment (or lack thereof), relationship stress, difficulty with establishing or maintaining healthy habits for an ageing body and a demanding life, and in some cases, the responsibility of parenting.

A COMPLEX PROBLEM FOR YOU

It's complicated for you as well! If your partner is struggling with a substance use problem, you face the reactions of friends, immediate family members (children of all ages), and extended family members: often including judgment, misunderstanding, punishment, fear, and "help" that can feel overbearing and shake your confidence. And when you are co-parenting with this partner, communication and effectively working together can be seriously tested under this stress.

But you *can* help. And we hope you keep reading.

MOTIVATION, CRAFT AND STRATEGIES FOR HELPING

There are variety of ways to help a loved one with a substance use problem. It is however, likely that you have not heard about them in spite of the evidence that they are enormously effective (as tested in rigorous research studies). Unfortunately, they have not been used widely in most treatment programs and have been completely neglected by the popular culture/media and they are why we wrote this guide! Because we want you to know about ALL of your options when it comes to helping your partner.

Researchers and clinicians over the past 40 years have developed and tested these tools and made them available (we describe many of them in our book *Beyond Addiction*). One of the most powerful is something called Motivational Interviewing developed by Dr. Bill Miller. It turns out that when it comes to making changes in behavior, motivation matters a lot! And contrary to what you may have been told or assumed, you, as a partner, can actually play a big role in helping your loved one shift their motivation towards positive change. There are of course things you can do or say that push things in exactly the opposite direction from what you want (i.e., confrontation, the silent treatment, forcing change). This 20 Minute Guide will expose you to a variety of skills you can use to turn motivation on and sustain it.

The second set of tools is called CRAFT (Community Reinforcement and Family Training) developed by Dr. Robert Meyers at the University of New Mexico. The CRAFT approach helps you think about the problem you face through a new behavioral perspective. It includes specific skills that will help you reinforce positive changes, communicate more effectively, and let consequences play a role, all while taking better care of yourself! It is the leading research-supported way for families to help their substance using loved ones. Compared to families trained to do interventions or who attend Al-Anon, family members who are trained in CRAFT are more likely to see their loved one's willingness to get help increase and substance use decrease or stop all together. In CRAFT, the concerned family member (that's you!) also feels better.

HOW TO USE THIS GUIDE

Unlike other approaches, CRAFT teaches you how to stay involved in a *positive, ongoing* way, while also taking care of yourself. This guide will help you with such tools as:

- How to react when your partner has been using substances and when he has NOT been using substances

- Getting more of what you want to see from your partner and less of what you don't

- How to talk to your partner so that you are more likely to be heard

- How to take care of yourself along the way

For each topic, we explain why it's important and how to use it to encourage change. We provide worksheets with examples to show you how CRAFT strategies look in action. We encourage you to use these worksheets to practice the skills as many times as you want or need. Feel free to skip around—it's not necessary to go through the topics in order, but it is important to practice each one.

We hope this is the beginning of positive change for you and your relationship. We appreciate the effort it takes to be a force for good. Thank you, truly. Take care of yourself, communicate, learn the CRAFT behavioral strategies, practice—and trust that things will change. Forty years of research and all our clinical experience says they will.

HELPING WITH UNDERSTANDING

To begin to deal effectively with any challenging problem, it's vital to understand the problem: where it came from, what contributes to keeping it in place, common features of the problem, how it is affecting you and those you love, and what to expect going forward. When you walk into a dark room, you need LIGHT so that you don't stumble around in the dark, banging yourself up and breaking things. We think of *Understanding* as the light you need to navigate the room you are in with your partner. Yes, action matters too! And this guide is loaded with suggestions about how to take effective action when it comes to helping, but *understanding* is the tool you need first to be effective with the rest.

We explore all of these topics much more fully in our book *Beyond Addiction; How Science and Kindness Help People Change*. In the 20 Minute Guide we cover the essentials of understanding, including a brief overview of new approaches for helping that have been supported by research studies over and over, as well as a discussion of the idea that *this struggle is different for each person and for each relationship they have*, and that finding your unique path is what matters. Next, we discuss the idea of "reinforcement", that people (your partner included) use substances for reasons. It is helpful to understand this fact as it will help you gain the important perspective that changing behavior is not so easy. Next, understanding the role of ambivalence (your partner wanting to change and NOT wanting to change), as well as providing some clarification about language you have probably heard (like "enabling") will take you even further down the path of thinking differently about the problem you face. We also review ways to think about conversations... how you talk about the problem with your partner, how to notice when it's going well, when it's not, and how to work with that. Last in this section on *Understanding* is a discussion of practice: these are new ideas and skills, and you'll need the time and patience (with yourself!) to practice all of these skills in order to be helpful to you and your partner. Why take the time to understand all of these new concepts? Because doing so will help you take more effective and strategic action to help your partner, which is what we know you want to do!

THIS SECTION INCLUDES SIX TOPICS:

1 One Answer Does Not Fit All
One Answer Does Not Fit All Worksheet

2 Behaviors Make Sense...Even Your Partner's
Behaviors Make Sense Worksheet

3 Warning! Ambivalence Is Normal

4 Enabling – An Overused Idea
Enabling – An Overused Idea Worksheet

5 Pay Attention to the Lights!

6 Practice, Practice, Practice! You Can't Get it Right Every Time

1. ONE ANSWER DOES NOT FIT ALL

"What should I do if my partner is drinking or using drugs?" The answer is that there are many answers, many paths, and many ways to help your partner change his relationship to substances. The answer for your partner will depend on the dynamics of your relationship and your partner as a unique individual. It will depend on what sorts of other problems he has, how long the behavior has been going on, who your/his friends are and what they think about substances, and about fifty other things. One size does not fit all. There are as many ways to change as there are people. It's a more complicated, perhaps unsettling answer than a universal solution, but worth grappling with because it's reality.

Improving family relations and friendships, reinforcing healthy habits, and introducing new interests are all helpful. Treatment and other therapeutic activities can help, and there are many options—some better supported by evidence than others, some more available and affordable than others, but altogether many possibilities to explore. In other words, in many ways your partner can get the help he needs.

If you are brave enough to ask for it, people will give you their opinions, advice, and even veiled criticism about helping your partner. You might hear, "How could you let that happen in your own house? He needs to go to rehab!" in one ear, and "It's not such a big deal, everybody overdoes it sometimes," in the other.

Whom should you listen to? What's the best advice? Again, no one size fits all **and** having a choice among treatment plans and plans for change in general predicts positive outcomes. *On these points the evidence is crystal clear:* giving people options helps them feel less trapped and invites them to get invested in the plan. This is also true for your partner.

So, as you think through ways to help your partner, do your homework. If the first (or fifth) person you consult tells you they know exactly what you should do, you might want to get some more opinions, especially if the person says this without meeting your partner. Black-and-white thinking abounds when it comes to figuring out how to deal with a substance use problem, and you may hear the range from "If you don't make him deal with this now, the next thing will be him landing in jail, or worse" to "It's just a little pot, what's the worry?" Falling into the black-and-white thinking trap can prevent you from understanding the subtleties of who your partner really is and how to help him. Give yourself permission to take the time you need to sort out what is going on and understand your options and try to be patient—with yourself and your partner.

After you collect information about your situation, we encourage you to trust *your* sense of what is best, putting aside your feelings of anger and self-doubt. Getting input is important, but you also need to trust what you know about your partner and your family.

A Suggestion: If you consider asking your partner to get a professional assessment, it may be helpful to describe it to him as a "consultation," which sounds less like "trapped in therapy forever." Ask around. Ask people you know about psychiatrists, psychologists, social workers, and so on that they liked. "The Top 100 Doctors" may not be the best place to start; the guy your friend from work liked might be a more appealing and accessible port in the storm.

ONE ANSWER DOES NOT FIT ALL: WORKSHEET

This week, make a list of all the advice you've gotten from other people about how to deal with your partner's substance use. Make note of the advice that triggers feelings or thoughts of self-doubt in you. Next to each one of those "triggers", list a potential alternative thought or coping response. This is an exercise in trusting yourself and practicing sifting through the feedback you'll get out in the world.

Trigger Comment	Alternative thought/Coping Response
"You should make him go to rehab."	I don't think he needs that intensive a treatment right now, and helping him make changes in the context of his normal life seems important.
"You should kick him out."	I'm not willing to kick him out right now—I can think of many steps to try before taking such drastic action.
"You should chill out. It's just pot."	I'm concerned because of the changes I see: lateness, fewer friends, quitting the gym, apathetic about things he used to care about.

2. BEHAVIORS MAKE SENSE...
EVEN YOUR PARTNER'S

If your partner is using drugs or alcohol, it's unlikely that they are simply being a "bad person" or *trying* to drive you crazy (although it feels like it). His behavior (in this case, substance use) is rewarding in some way — emotionally, physically, socially, or perhaps all of the above. In psychology we call this "reinforcement," and it applies to motivation and change in all of us. People take action—work hard at a job, work out at the gym, smoke pot—and repeat that action because they get something from doing it. Getting a raise, feeling physically fit, or having less anxiety is the reward or "reinforcer" for the action, the reason they keep doing it. Generally, people do not persist in a behavior (for very long) unless it affords some benefit.

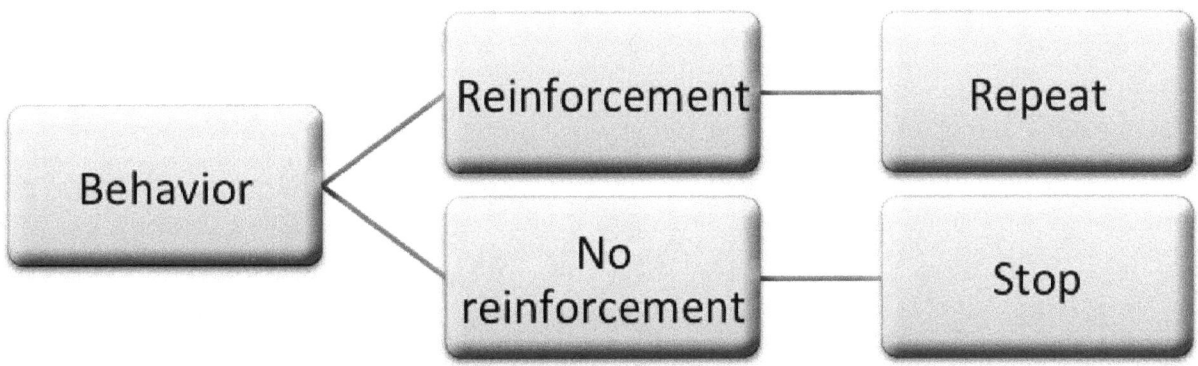

Feeling relaxed, exhilarated, less anxious, braver, funnier, part of the group, are all potential *benefits* of using substances. If there were no benefits, there would be no use. This is important because knowing what, in particular, your partner gets from using substances provides clues about *what could happen instead*. For example, if you think that your partner is drinking in part because it helps him take a break from his hectic work schedule, you can come up with other, healthy ways he might be able to get those breaks. You might decide to schedule more down-time or relax some of the pressure you notice he's feeling at home.

Understanding what your partner gets from using can also lower your fear and anxiety, as it makes the behavior less random and more predictable. If he drinks as a "social lubricant" when socializing with both work colleagues and friends, then you know he's more at risk when he's out socializing than home with the family. Knowing this won't eliminate your anxiety completely, but it can reduce it. And as you learn CRAFT strategies, you will be equipped to intervene constructively to influence the patterns.

Finally, understanding your partner's reinforcers will help you empathize with him. Why would you want to empathize with non-constructive or destructive behavior? It will help you take it less personally (as in, "how can he do this to us?!"), and feel less angry and more connected, which will give you energy for helping him change. Instead of thinking he is irresponsible or torturing you, you can see the underlying loneliness, insecurity, depression, or boredom, which are all things you can help your partner address. In turn, and even more importantly, understanding your partner's behavior instead of just being upset about it can help *him* feel understood, which will make him more likely to collaborate on a plan for change.

BEHAVIORS MAKE SENSE...
WORKSHEET

In order to promote positive activities that can compete with your partner's use of substances, you'll need to understand what is reinforcing for him about his use. In this exercise, we ask you to brainstorm what your partner may like about using substances. If this is distressing, bear in mind, his reasons to use are clues pointing towards reasons to do something else instead. If you're still not convinced of the value of this exercise, or you just need a break from it, you may want to read the chapter on motivation in our book, *Beyond Addiction*.

Step 1: List any reasons why your partner may be using substances. Start with reasons s/he has told you in the past ("it relaxes me," "all my colleagues drink a lot," etc.) and also include reasons you believe from your own observations. Try to avoid blaming or accusatory reasons ("because he's an idiot," "because he doesn't care about anything," "he's trying to piss me off.")

Step 2: Outline the basic needs that each reason in Step 1 fulfills. Below is a list of potential needs, and you can add others.

Stress reduction	Anxiety relief
Enjoyment	Social interaction
Mood stabilizing	Risk taking or thrill
Rebellion	

Step 3: Once you have identified underlying reasons why your partner might be using substances, brainstorm alternative ways you could help him/her to address that issue.

Reasons for Use	Basic Needs Being Met	Alternatives
"Everyone else is drinking a lot."	Social comfort, maybe anxiety relief.	Talk to doctor about anxiety; help plan other social events.
"I just need to chill out after work."	Stress reduction.	Give time to unwind after work without immediately starting responsibilities.

Reasons for Use	Basic Needs Being Met	Alternatives

The Partner's 20 Minute Guide

3. WARNING! AMBIVALENCE IS NORMAL

Sometimes change will make sense to your partner, other times it won't. He may give reasons for change one day (green lights); and the next day he argues against it (red lights). This motivational seesaw *is normal*—it's how ambivalence gets expressed and is par for the course in virtually any kind of change, from dieting to ending relationships to changing careers, not just changing substance use.

Why might your partner feel ambivalent, when the costs seem so clear to you? The change you hope for may have its benefits, but remember, your partner gets something from using substances (it's reinforcing!). As a result, sometimes using or not changing makes sense. Changing that behavior requires learning a new behavior to replace it, and the work involved in learning can be hard and uncomfortable.

Change can be understood as a **cost-benefit equation**, as illustrated by the (less loaded) example below.

Reasons to Exercise/Change (Benefits)	Reasons to Not Exercise/Not Change (Costs)
• Better health	• Feel really awkward in the gym socially
• Increased energy	• Like extra time at home
• Doctor will be happy	• Get fatigued from exercise
• Feel better about myself	• Reminds me how out of shape I am
	• Don't want to pay for gym

This is ambivalence: wanting to go in two directions at the same time, often with good (or good enough) reasons either way. If you listen carefully, you can hear your partner's ambivalence in the way he talks about his experiences and decisions. Try to appreciate that his reasons for both changing a behavior and not changing it are reasonable—and don't take the bait! Arguing with ambivalence or trying to make him see your side is just begging for him to defend his reasons for *not* changing. If you react to "I don't want to change" (red light talk) by arguing, trying to shout it down or lecturing ("what do you mean you don't want to stop, you could jeopardize your job because of it!"), you are probably going to get a defensive response (yelling back or better yet, door slamming). And, you may miss hearing the other more subtle examples of your partner's desire to change ("I don't want to miss that soccer game in the morning").

Not getting into an argument gives him room to reflect on his own reasons to change. Instead of fighting with ambivalence, you can gently guide his behavior with your responses. You can choose to respond with communication and behavioral strategies that help tip the scale toward change. Patience can come in very handy!

4. ENABLING - AN OVERUSED IDEA

...am I enabling?

The focus in the 20 Minute Guide is on your **active, positive participation** and **engagement** with your partner. There is a reason for this! The Guide is grounded in the behaviorally-oriented strategies of CRAFT and Motivational Interviewing and encourages a collaborative, "involved" approach. By learning new ways of interacting, you can be in a powerful position to influence profound, real, and lasting change in your partner. However, several words of clarification are in order here:

"Enabling"... "Co-dependent"... "Powerless"... "Loving detachment"... These are words and ideas you are likely to hear as you navigate your relationship and your partner's relationship with substances. While these ideas are meant to help families understand this struggle, they are often confusing and at times used in ways that are shaming and discouraging. In brief, here is the chain of commonly held ideas about substance abuse, which can leave you feeling trapped and blamed:

- **Idea #1**: substance abuse is caused by flaws in *character, morals*, and *genetics*; your partner is "powerless" to control his use and you are "powerless" to help

- **Idea #2**: your partner's reluctance or trouble in deciding to change is evidence of their "denial" rather than natural ambivalence about change

- **Idea #3**: attempts by you to help are "enabling"; that is, involvement on your part is actually *helping them to keep using*. You will often get the message that *any* love or kindness toward a substance-using partner is "enabling"

- **Idea #4**: the recommended path is to "detach with love" (the "Anon" programs) or to force compliance "lovingly" (e.g. have an Intervention)

Within this framework, the only options to this very frustrating, painful and scary situation can seem to be either: a) walking away and "taking care of yourself" while you wait for your partner to "hit rock bottom" or b) confronting your partner with some type of forced choice (as in an intervention, where the answer is "you're going away"). Unfortunately, being told that you are powerless in relation to your partner's use OR being put in the role of *forcing* change goes against what the evidence shows us: neither of these responses are likely to be effective in changing your partner's behavior in a sustained way.

SO...WHAT DOES WORK?

Reinforcing positive behavior: the critical link

What the evidence (and experience) ***does*** support is something very different: you can ***stay involved*** with your partner, ***influence them positively*** to change, and ***take care of yourself***! The relationship you have with your partner is in fact a powerful force for positive change. It is under your control, and it does not need to include forcing compliance, withdrawing, or neglecting yourself. If you have been taught that any involvement on your part will only make things worse (is "enabling"), this idea of active involvement – "taking the driver's seat" – will seem like a bad idea! But it's not....and you can take care of yourself at the same time.

The strategies you will learn in the 20 Minute Guide are based on the CRAFT and Motivational Interviewing approaches, and encourage you to stay actively involved with your partner's ***non-using, positive behaviors***, the behaviors you WANT to encourage. These strategies include noticing, praising, and rewarding (called "reinforcing") ***constructive*** behaviors, the ones that you would like to see more of (especially behaviors that directly "compete" with substance use), and NOT reinforcing the destructive (substance using) behaviors, the ones that you no longer want to see. Developing a lifestyle that competes with substance use is one of the most natural and effective ways to reinforce sustainable, positive change...and you are in a unique position to help create this lifestyle.

"Enabling" revisited: So what IS enabling? Enabling is acting in ways that reinforce or support (not purposefully) substance use/negative behaviors. Examples include calling work for your hungover partner to (falsely) explain their absence, or giving them money to help them "get by" when they run out due to their use. Often, this is an attempt to "saw off the rough edges" for your partner, a very natural parental impulse, but one that prevents your partner from learning the "naturally occurring" outcomes of their own choices and actions.

On the other hand, actively reinforcing positive behaviors, the positive behaviors that you would like to see more of, is not enabling. The ***Helping with Actions*** section of the 20 Minute Guide includes many ways for you to practice being active, involved, and helpful...in ways that reinforce and increase the likelihood of positive behavior change. This is actually the **opposite** of "enabling."

Points to remember:

1. You can make a difference! In any big change process, it's understandable to at times feel stuck in the thoughts about all the things you wish you'd done differently in the past. Also, when scared and feeling mistreated, positive reinforcement does not come easily! Know that you **can** influence change, and even consider how you can positively reinforce *yourself* in the process of making these changes.

2. Taking an active role does NOT make you an "enabler." The issue is not whether you are being active, but ***what type of behaviors you are reinforcing*** (see "The Gardener's Dilemma" below)

3. "You catch more flies with honey than vinegar." Just as it is easier to attract flies with sweet honey than sour vinegar, it is easier to get your partner to listen with loving words than with criticism. And this is more than a wise old saying; it is proven by research!

4. You have another chance! Changing your behavior can be difficult, but it's helpful to remember that you get to keep trying and practicing. Be patient with yourself. You have a lot of time and energy invested in this relationship – you've likely tried to help your loved one change many times. Isn't it worth it to try another approach?

5. Change does not usually happen overnight! A common experience is to feel so afraid, angry, and desperate that you make ultimatums you're not actually ready or willing to follow through with when it comes down to it. Also, you might feel discouraged if your efforts to positively reinforce healthy behaviors do not result in changes right away. Baby steps! With this approach, you are learning to focus on making small improvements to your own self care (so that you have more resources and feel less desperate) and to improve and increase the positive interactions between you and your partner (to improve your relationship and help you feel less angry). Small changes build confidence and create the foundation for substantive, long-lasting change.

The Gardener's Dilemma - A gardener strives to plant, grow, and care for a healthy garden, with many plants of varying colors and sizes. The garden, however, includes plants you want to see and unfortunately plants showing up that you don't want to see (e.g. weeds). Every garden needs water to help nourish, grow, and strengthen the good plants. But what to do about those weeds? Some may suggest cutting off the sprinkler system. In not watering the garden, surely the weeds will vanish? But at what cost? The weeds may disappear, but what happens to the plants you would like to nourish? The weeds may also come back stronger since they are adept at growing in harsh conditions. Others may suggest watering the whole garden *more*; perhaps the plants you want will grow faster than the weeds? And the cost of this? By watering everything, the weeds will more than likely also grow stronger (enabling). Our wise gardener steps back and makes a decision: to water more strategically, being careful to water the plants you want to see grow, and keeping a careful eye to keep the water away from the weeds. While this watering approach make take some practice and effort to develop (and to be able to tell a tomato from a weed!), it offers the promise of growing a garden full of healthy plants.

ENABLING - AN OVERUSED IDEA: WORKSHEET

The exercise below will test your understanding of the difference between positive reinforcement actions and "enabling" actions. For each row, take the reinforcement action (or the enabling action) that is given and fill in the missing action. Sample answers are on the next page.

Positive reinforcement actions:	"Enabling" actions:
Your wife gets home on time and sober (though perhaps this is not common). You know she hasn't eaten dinner yet and you offer to warm something up for her.	
	Your boyfriend is struggling to keep his job, in part because of his substance use. You let him know that it's okay for him to quit his job to study for exams ahead.
Your partner is not supporting himself financially, in part because of the money he spends on substances. Because you believe exercise will compete with his bad habits and possibly improve his mental health, you agree to pay for his gym membership.	
	Your girlfriend got in a fight with her sister and knowing how badly she feels and how much she wants an escape from those feelings, you tell her it's okay that she drink at home.
Your husband is using substances off and on. You decide to continue a tradition of Sunday morning pancakes with the family as long as he arrives clear-headed to the meal.	

ANSWER KEY

Positive reinforcement actions:	"Enabling" actions:
Your wife gets home on time and sober (though perhaps this is not common). You know she hasn't eaten dinner yet and you offer to warm something up for her.	Your wife comes home at night and although she seems intoxicated and is too late to join the family for dinner, you worry she hasn't eaten, so you warm up a meal for her.
Your boyfriend is struggling to keep his job, partly due to substance use, but also other factors. When sober, he asks you to help him plan for how he can ask to have a reduced work week while he studies for an exam, and you agree to help him think about how to make this request.	Your boyfriend is struggling to keep his job, in part because of his substance use. You let him know that it's okay for him to quit his job to study for exams ahead.
Your partner is not supporting himself financially, in part because of the money he spends on substances. Because you believe exercise will compete with his bad habits and possibly improve his mental health, you agree to pay for his gym membership.	Your partner does not make enough money to support himself, in part because he spends so much money on substances. You "supplement" him at the end of each month with extra cash.
Your girlfriend got in a fight with her sister. She comes to you sober, but distraught, and you comfort her with a hug and offer to talk. (Refraining from telling her things you do not believe, eg. Not telling her she is blameless.)	Your girlfriend got in a fight with her sister and knowing how badly she feels and how much she wants an escape from those feelings, you tell her it's okay that she drink at home.
Your husband is using substances off and on. You decide to continue a tradition of Sunday morning pancakes with the family as long as he arrives clear-headed to the meal.	On mornings after your husband has stayed up late using substances, you make pancakes for him no matter how late he gets up.

5. PAY ATTENTION TO THE LIGHTS!

Good communication starts with this overarching goal: to stay connected and keep moving forward. You have, no doubt, already tried to talk to your partner (or shout at, plead with, etc.) about changing her behavior. We'd guess you have started many a conversation with great intentions only to see them go off course and become unproductive or downright destructive.

Imagine if there were traffic signals in conversation to tell you when to stop or go; to help you get safely to your destination. Actually, if you know what to look for, there are:

The light is **green** when your partner is positively engaged with you, willing to listen and respond constructively, and maybe, though not necessarily, talking about change.

The light is **red** when your partner is destructively engaged with you (yelling, cursing, going silent), not listening, and probably moving away from the idea of change. For example when she is defending her use of substances.

That may sound obvious, but when you *pay attention* to these lights and respond accordingly, you are much more likely to get somewhere and avoid harm along the way. Here are some examples.

You: "I'd like to talk to you about not drinking at the party tonight."

Your partner:

Green Lights	Red Lights
"Okay, but can we not have a fight about it?" "Can I tell you what I think?" "I won't drink, I have work early in the morning."	"You just want to push your prudish rules on me." "Why do you always overreact?" "I hate when you try to dictate how I behave with our friends."

Red lights are frustrating, especially when you're in a rush to see change. You may be tempted to "gun it" and try to force your way through. But you know from experience that ignoring red lights is dangerous: people end up fighting, saying things they regret, feeling worse instead of better, and no closer to positive change—in fact, often further from it.

Paying attention to the lights will help you stay oriented to the goal of communication: you want it to go forward. You don't want to crash.

What follows are strategies and approaches to communicating that will allow for more green lights than red, as well as ways to notice those red lights, so you can stop and try again.

A Side Note: Take a moment to notice Red and Green lights in conversation with anyone. When you don't jump to taking a side, you will find people consider both sides more easily. When you strongly advocate for only one side, notice how quickly the other person picks up the opposite side of the argument.

The Partner's 20 Minute Guide

6. PRACTICE, PRACTICE, PRACTICE!
YOU CAN'T GET IT RIGHT EVERY TIME...

At moments, as you read this guide you may have the thought, "but I've tried this before and it didn't work." Maybe so, but if you are like many people in this struggle, perhaps you have not been able to combine the consistency, timing, collaboration, and persistence that gets results.

Taking part in this change process means you're learning too. Take pride when something goes better because of an effort you made to change, and be kind to yourself and patient with your partner when it doesn't. Learning any new thing takes practice, whether it's positive communication, golf, or figuring out your new phone. At first, most of us feel awkward, even "bad at it." As you practice with CRAFT, you might get frustrated and be tempted to give up. You might say to yourself, "this isn't working," "this isn't me, or "I can't do this and my partner doesn't care anyway." Such thoughts and impulses are normal when you're learning; that is, they are *part of the process*, not reason to quit.

As in all learning, *wanting* to know the skill doesn't get you the skill; practice does. Practice again and again. Experiment and learn from the data you collect, and adjust your plans accordingly. Track your practice to create a record you can look back on, to help you remember what you're doing, when you're doing it, and how it's actually going—which might be different from how it feels like it's going on a bad day. By tracking you can make connections between your effort and its effects on the wellbeing of your partner, your family, and yourself.

Developing your helping skills will take time and patience. Helping your partner change through your relationship will be a process. Give yourself room to practice, make mistakes, and not get discouraged. You will get better at the changes you are trying to make, and so will your partner.

***Beyond Addiction: How Science and Kindness Help People Change (A Guide for Families)* is available from Scribner in bookstores near you and online at beyondaddictionbook.com.**

CHAPTER III

HELPING WITH SELF CARE

In this guide we prioritize "taking care of yourself" because it is critically important to helping effectively and helping for the long term. Having a partner struggling with substance use is incredibly stressful, and has the capacity to wear everyone down, losing your patience, balance, and resilience.

In this section, we focus on three important aspects of taking care of yourself:
1) understanding the stress of this situation and developing concrete ways to relieve that stress,
2) being aware of your emotional states, in particular your very natural negative emotions, and learning to effectively manage them, 3) finding ways to get support and avoid isolation, and
4) managing the very painful feeling of shame.

THIS SECTION INCLUDES FOUR TOPICS:

1
This Is Really Stressful!
This Is Really Stressful! Worksheet

2
Manage Your Emotions
Manage Your Emotions Worksheet

3
You're Not Alone
You're Not Alone Worksheet

4
Shame and Self-Compassion: Opposite Worlds
Shame and Self-Compassion Worksheet

1. THIS IS REALLY STRESSFUL!

If you love someone with a substance use problem, worry, frustration, and feelings of helplessness probably consume large amounts of your time and energy. As you focus on your partner, taking care of yourself probably falls to the bottom of your list, if it makes the list at all. You might reason that you and your family will feel better when your partner gets better, so it makes sense to prioritize his needs at your (and perhaps the rest of the family's) expense for now. This impulse to suspend paying attention to your own health and happiness is understandable but is likely to cause more problems than you realize if it causes you to be reactive, anxious, or easily frustrated. Your partner is struggling with a variety of issues and your ability to stay mostly calm and optimistic will help both of you. It will also help if you are sleeping, eating well, and finding some comfort and joy in your life. And it helps if you don't hang your wellbeing on his or have your health and outlook on life be dependent on the choices your partner makes.

Taking care of yourself is vital to helping your partner and the rest of your family. Try to resist the impulse to put your life on hold and live only in emergency/panic mode. How can you possibly go to a movie when you're worried that your partner might be out at the bar again?! Well, what if taking a break from worrying is the most helpful thing you could do right now, *and you can learn how*?

Remember the safety announcement on planes before takeoff: secure your own oxygen mask first before you help someone else. This is for the benefit of the whole group. Helping works the same way on the ground. You need a certain amount of "oxygen" (sleep, nutrition, exercise, socializing, and fun) to sustain you as you help your partner. Without attention to your own needs, you risk collapsing before you manage to help. Even if you stay standing, you won't be able to think, plan, act, and troubleshoot as effectively as you can when you're healthy, optimistic, and resilient. The strategies suggested in the CRAFT approach require that you approach problems with clarity and consistency, which is nearly impossible to do if you are physically or emotionally exhausted.

WHAT IS RESILIENCE?

Resilience is how you "roll with" life; it's how you adapt to change and what flexibility and creativity you can muster for solving problems. It is the point of self-care and without resilience, over time, you become less able to tolerate disappointments with your partner without sinking into despair or lashing back with anger. As you try to help your partner change, tension with your partner will likely rise (if their desire to change is low or as they struggle to change, etc.). If you react to that tension with high emotion (anger, despair, panic), it will make it harder for you to be an effective helper and make your partner more resistant to being helped.

Depending on the severity of your situation, you may not feel like there's room for anything other than reacting to the latest crisis. We encourage you to look at it another way - you can't afford *not* to take care of yourself. Though people sometimes change "overnight," it usually takes longer. Even when there's an Ah-Ha moment, the real work of sustaining change is ongoing (if you've ever made a New Year's resolution, you know this). Helping your partner change her relationship to substances will likely be a long-term project that's better approached as a marathon rather than a sprint. You'll need to keep up your energy reserves and pace yourself. You'll need to prepare for hills, weather, and competition. Even if your situation improves fairly quickly—and we hope it does—you'll be more helpful if you bring your best self to it. It's not "touchy-feely" to take care of yourself; it's tactical.

Suffocating from worry, fear, anger, resentment, or stress will not help you help someone else. You need "oxygen" *continuously* to be the best support possible for your partner. We recommend that you spend time *each week* doing something that makes you feel good, relaxed, content, and soothed—something you want to do as opposed to something you think you should do.

How will you contribute to your own self-care this week? Consider your health (nutrition, sleep, exercise) as well as what nourishes you intellectually, emotionally, and spiritually. In case it's been so long since you've entertained the notion of doing what you'd like to do that you've forgotten, we've included a list of possibilities at the end of this worksheet.

Step 1: Identify areas of your life that need attention, where a change would help you feel less stressed or improve the overall quality of your life. The following questions may help you think about this:

- How do you feel about your <u>intellectual wellbeing</u>? (Have you felt cut off or disengaged from matters that used to interest you? When was the last time you learned something new? Had a discussion about something other than your partner's problems?)

- How do you feel about your <u>physical health</u>? (How are you sleeping? When was the last time you exercised? Have you found yourself eating poorly? When was the last time you had a check-up?)

- How do you feel about your <u>emotional wellbeing</u>? (Have you been more emotionally reactive lately (short fuse, quick to cry etc.)? Do you find that you are feeling numb, shut down, angry? Are you doing or saying things that don't match who you want to be?)

- How do you feel about <u>your own use of substances</u>? (We're not saying that using any substances on your part is necessarily problematic for your partner, but it will have an impact— along with everything else you do. Practically, your partner may feel permitted or even invited by the presence and availability of substances. Emotionally, even as peers, you model for each other how feelings are managed: how you pick yourself up, knock yourself out, handle the pressure, or blow off steam. Would change on your part help support change on his part?

Step 2: Pick an area (from above) and brainstorm possible solutions: what you'd like to accomplish related to your self-care and why it would help you build the resiliency you need to help your partner.

What I would like to accomplish…	Why it would help me…
I would like to sleep through the night.	It would help me feel less irritable in the morning, when we often fight.
I would like to find the time to read a good book.	It would help me take a break and feel less resentful about spending all my time worrying about my partner.
Your ideas:	

Steps 3: Select (e.g., by process of elimination or because they jump out at you) two solutions and convert them into doable goals (remember: keep them brief, simple, positive, specific and measurable, reasonable and achievable, in your control, and involving skills you already have or are learning). Set two self-care goals for the coming week. We recommend at least one of them be something that's entirely enjoyable to you.

To improve my self-care, this week I will: _____

_____.

Example: *I will go for a run 2 times this week to blow off steam and feel more tired when I go to bed. This will help me sleep better.*

To increase joy in my life, I will: _____

_____.

Example: *I will go to the bookstore on my way home from work and buy a new book. Then I will stop doing chores at 10:00 and get lost in my book.*

Step 4: Identify obstacles that could interfere with your "goals of the week."

Obstacles to Practicing this Goal	Coping Skills for Handling Obstacles
It's hard to find time to go for a run.	Plan out the week and schedule time for runs around other activities. Commit to it like an appointment.
I'm too worried to sit and read. I get distracted.	Take deep breaths and give myself permission to start small. If I can read for 15 minutes, that's better than no break at all.

There are many ways to tend to your mind, body, heart, and soul. We include this by-no-means complete list to help you brainstorm your way to better self-care.*

- Visit with a friend (face-to-face, on the phone, by email, etc.).

- Cook your favorite meal.

- Go out to eat your favorite meal or eat a "comfort food" that you find soothing.

- Take a class in a topic that interests you.

- Let yourself space out and watch TV.

- Go to a movie.

- Watch hilarious videos on YouTube.

- Get a manicure, pedicure, or massage.

- Go for a walk or run. Let yourself take in the sounds and smells. Try to be present.

- Go for a hike (even in the city). Walk somewhere you have never been before. Take in the "newness" of your surroundings.

- Engage in a sport (either alone or with people) that you enjoy (swimming, golf, biking, tennis, yoga, basketball, bowling...).

- Do an activity that gets your adrenaline pumping (rock climbing, skydiving, roller coasters, horseback riding, karaoke singing).

- Take a nap; let yourself doze off.

- Sincerely compliment or appreciate another person (this could be a stranger).

- Play cards; do brain teasers, crosswords, word games.

- Listen to music you enjoy.

- Get a haircut.

- Help someone out.

- Take your dog for a walk; play with a pet.

- Sit outside and watch the clouds for ten minutes; sit in a park and watch the birds and squirrels.

- Watch a live sporting event or go hear some live music.

- Visit an exhibit at a museum or wander around a gallery.

- Go for a drive.

- Lift weights, take a class at the gym, and hire a trainer for a few sessions.

- Listen to a podcast.

- Go to a bookstore or magazine store. Read something for pleasure.

- Go to services at your usual place of worship.

- Go to services not at your usual place of worship.

- Give time to a hobby you enjoy (photography, knitting, gardening, cooking, painting…).

- Meditate; download a guided mindfulness training.

- Buy your favorite flowers; don't forget to smell them.

- Re-read a favorite book, poem, or article. Sit and flip through a magazine.

- Draw a picture; doodle.

- Spend an hour window-shopping; visit a flea market.

- Drink a cup of tea or coffee while doing nothing else.

- Volunteer for an afternoon or evening.

- Take a bath; light your favorite candle.

- Write yourself a nice note that you can read again and again.

- Make a photo album.

- Do a puzzle.

- Take a day trip; plan a trip.

- Play an instrument; learn a new song.

- Dress in your favorite outfit; buy yourself something you have wanted to wear.

- Visit your favorite coffee shop.

- Buy yourself an ice cream cone.

- Notice! At the end of each day for a week (or a month), jot down three things you enjoyed today (noticing really helps).

For more ideas and a thorough self-care assessment, see the self-care chapters of our book, *Beyond Addiction*, especially the "You Are Here" exercise.

---

*   Adapted from pp 157-159 in: Linehan, Marsha, M (1993). Skills Training Manual for Treating Borderline Personality Disorder. London: Guilford Press.

2. MANAGE YOUR EMOTIONS

Many people's level of happiness is determined by the emotional state of their primary relationship. It can be difficult to enjoy yourself in any way or have hope for the future if you feel your relationship is in conflict, and this is especially true if substance use is present. You may find yourself yelling and even screaming, nagging, begging, crying, or just shutting down. At times, you may feel like giving up completely.

Two things about these feelings: 1) they are normal, and 2) you weren't born knowing how to deal with the situation you are facing, but you can learn. Managing these negative feelings is an important job to take on, as they needn't prevent you from helping your partner or enjoying yourself, the rest of your family, and the other parts of your life.

YOUR NEGATIVE EMOTIONS

When your partner is using substances or engaging in other risky behaviors, you will naturally feel afraid, angry, betrayed, ashamed, confused, guilty, and a host of other painful emotions. Your task is to manage them so you don't act on them with your partner.

Acknowledging your feelings to yourself as they happen helps defuse them, though it may seem counterintuitive. Just the act of being aware can help keep your negative emotions from bursting out of you in the form of confrontational or hostile behaviors that push away your partner and take you further from your ultimate goals. Awareness gives you choice and helps you change course to be most effective. If you know you are about ready to boil over, you can step back and decide to finish a conversation in the morning when cooler heads prevail. If you know you are on the verge of panic, you can ask another loved one or friend for support. Oftentimes, letting your negative feelings simply *be* allows them to pass, as they do when you don't fan the flames or act on them, giving you quicker access to the positive emotions you need to help your partner change. (Remember why you're reading this in the first place: you *love* this person. That's where help comes from.)

THE IMPACT OF EMOTIONS ON YOUR BEHAVIOR

Acting on your emotions by breaking down, confronting, or detaching is counterproductive in many ways. Let us count them: 1) you ultimately feel worse (for losing control, for saying things you regret); 2) you help your partner divert attention from their actions by making you the problem ("my husband tries to control me," "my wife is hysterical and always overreacts"); 3) your partner may cope with the negative feelings brought on by the situation by turning to substances more (this is *not* to blame you for your partner's behavior, but to help you do everything you can to remove yourself as her excuse); 4) a truth about motivation: confrontation leads to resistance and your partner's motivation is likely to drop; and 5) as your relationship deteriorates due to conflict or detachment, so does your positive influence.

The alternative to acting on your negative feelings is to manage them and find ways to be calm and non-confrontational. Engaging with your partner in this way does not mean you are passively accepting risky behavior; it means your partner will be more likely to hear what you think about the behavior and, more importantly, about healthier ways to behave. Staying connected in a calmer way also lets her know you care (whatever she says in the heat of the moment, trust that she cares that you care) and are prepared to stay the course. Not least, you will be modeling the behavior you want to see from your partner – positive actions like this can be contagious.

Easier said than done, right?

HOW TO MANAGE

- Take care of yourself. Do at least the minimum to keep up your resilience—enough sleep, a balanced diet, exercise, and so on—and then some: time to yourself, activities you enjoy, time with people who make you laugh and feel loved, and so on.

- Anticipate your negative emotions. How does your partner push your buttons? What triggers your anger, yelling, and other unproductive behaviors? Make a list; then read on to learn some other ways to respond.

- In your head, label your feelings and describe to yourself what's happening: "I feel really angry incredibly fast when he uses that disrespectful tone with me." Just narrating to yourself what's happening can provide a little bit of distance between you and your emotional reaction.

- Take a "time out." Give yourself permission to avoid the most triggering situations while you try to improve the climate in your home.

- Remember that this behavior that sets you off is most likely *not* designed to hurt you or make you crazy, as much as it might feel that way. You may understandably wish she thought more about your feelings before acting this way, but most likely she is feeling pretty out of control, and remembering that this is not behavior personally designed to drive you nuts can help you get through the moment.

- Set a limit. If, upon reflection, you choose not to put up with a particular behavior (such as name-calling or swearing, yelling or physical aggression), plan what the consequences will be and use the communication skills in this guide and in our book, *Beyond Addiction*, to explain this to your partner in advance. In a calm moment, you might say, "I know it's hard for you to keep from swearing when you're mad, but if you start swearing like that in the future, I'm going to excuse myself and go to bed."

> Remember your goals: You want your partner to change her relationship with substances and you want her to eventually make the changes for reasons that matter to her. By staying connected you can be a positive influence and help her find those reasons.

This exercise will help you recognize what triggers your negative emotions and behaviors, so you can be ready with a more helpful—or at least non-harmful—response. In the left-hand column, list everything you can think of that your partner does that pushes your buttons and makes you more likely to act on your negative emotions. Then, in the right-hand column, plan an alternative coping response. Choose one coping response to practice this week.

Trigger	Coping Response
He comes home obviously under the influence.	This week, I will practice resisting the urge to talk to him when he comes home under the influence; instead, I will go to a place in our home where I don't see him and where I can focus on something else.
He ignores me/takes a really dismissive tone with me when I ask how his day went.	This week, I will go in my room, relax, and tell myself I can talk to him more effectively tomorrow when I'm calmer.
Your ideas:	

3. YOU'RE NOT ALONE: REDUCING ISOLATION

You may wonder if anyone can really understand what you're going through. The truth is that your path is unique. Some of what happens could only happen in your family. Yet millions of people have walked down similar roads; roads with stories, realizations, experiences, heartbreaks, and successes that look, sound, and feel a lot like what you're going through.

We recommend talking to some of these people. Research has found time and again that social support helps when it comes to, well, pretty much everything. You may worry about privacy, gossip, and the "public" perception of your partner/yourself/your family. You might not consciously choose to withdraw; you may simply be rushing around with your heart in your throat, and your focus has naturally turned inward. You may feel protective of your partner; and frankly, at times, embarrassed. These feelings can easily lead you to pull away from the support systems you normally rely on. Or you may not be in the habit of asking for help. You may even be dead-set against it.

While these are reasonable concerns and valid feelings, isolation can make you feel worse over time, depriving you of the energy and resiliency you need to cope—and to help. Do not underestimate the toll that isolation can take. It can exacerbate depression, anxiety, and stress, making it more difficult for you to handle hard, emotionally charged situations. Over time, your buffer zone (or emotional resilience) gets smaller and smaller; your ability to take another disappointment from your partner, be it small (late from work), medium (late or misses a parenting event) or large (crashed the car) without sinking or reacting badly yourself gets really diminished.

Conversely, social support can increase your resilience. You are not alone, but isolation can creep up on you. Fighting the pull toward isolation will help you feel better, and help you help better.

The Partner's 20 Minute Guide

YOU'RE NOT ALONE: WORKSHEET

How could you connect with another person or people this week? Keep in mind, support has many faces and you may have different needs at different times. Consider who in your life might be useful to confide in, but also who is good at having fun, making you laugh, distracting you, or helping you relax. Reaching out to others doesn't have to mean pouring out your heart (though if that is what you need right now, go for it). Taking time out from your problems is as important as talking them through.

Even if you don't feel like isolation is a big factor right now, try to do something social at least once a week to see if it helps. "Something social" can be as simple as a phone chat with your sister or as elaborate as a dinner with friends.

Step 1: Identify people in your life who fill different needs for you. (Some people may fit in more than one category.)

Good Listener:	
Good Advice Giver:	
Just for Fun/ Makes Me Laugh:	
Cheerleader/ Encourages Me:	
Confidant:	
Playmate/Likes to Do Things with Me:	
Shoulder to Cry On:	

<u>Step 2</u>: Look over your answers to Step 1 and pick a person you'd like to see this week. Think about what kind of socializing you'd most prefer right now—who and why. Then brainstorm how you could connect with the person this coming week.

I need someone who is: _____

I want to spend time with:_____

I would like to do*: _____

---
*   For this line include specifics like *when* you would like to meet the person and *what* you would like to do with him or her.

Step 3: Identify obstacles that could interfere with meeting your goal(s) for connecting with others this week. Then, come up with a strategy to address each one of these barriers and maximize your chances of accomplishing your goal.

Obstacles to achieving my goal	Coping strategy for dealing with the obstacles
It's hard to find time.	Ask for help with household chores to free up some time during the evenings. Schedule a "date" in advance so that we have it on the calendar.
My friend might not be available.	Have a back-up plan in case she's not free. Call her a week in advance so that she has a better chance of making herself available.

4. SHAME AND SELF COMPASSION: OPPOSITE WORLDS

Sometimes it's a small nagging voice…sometimes it's a thundering judgement…but it may well be a tiring, painful accompaniment in your head these days: "It's me…my husband's struggles with substances are my fault." There are many versions of this internal dialogue:

"If I had only been more (or less)…"

"If I had just let her…"

"I should have talked him out of going on those medications"

"Why didn't I say something when I first suspected?"

When your partner is struggling with substance use issues, it is normal to rethink paths you have taken. Feeling regret about all the pain everyone is in is also natural. There is, however, another very common emotion that is not so helpful, and is in fact extraordinarily painful, and that is *shame*.

Shame is a complicated, intensely uncomfortable, and "sticky" emotion (meaning it grabs on and is hard to shake off). It usually comes about in response to something you feel you have done wrong or reactions you have had that you feel bad about. It includes feeling exposed, vulnerable, unsure and sometimes humiliated and it ends up feeling like it's "**who you are**." In contrast to the dull ache of regret, shame has a sharp, cutting edge that makes no distinction between reasonable and unreasonable. It makes teasing apart what you have done well, and what you might do differently almost impossible, as everything is thrown in the same basket and seen as bad, your fault, and unforgivable.

While shame is usually about one's own actions/thoughts, your partner's actions, feelings, and experiences expose you to feeling shame **for** them, **about** them **and** about yourself. The worst pain? Feeling ashamed of feeling ashamed about your partner. This is not semantics, but the real experience of loving someone with a substance problem. It's not fair, but it is intense and real, and a burden worth reckoning with.

As a partner, there are any number of pathways leading to feeling shame. One of the most common is guilt about things that you have said out of anger or confusion (e.g., "I can't believe you are a drug addict!" or "You are a disgrace"). Another is feelings of misgiving about how things were handled (e.g., "I wasn't around enough" or "I was too hard on him...I didn't know he was depressed") or decisions that were made along the way (e.g., letting drug use go unaddressed early on). Shame can also come from the stigma associated with substance use problems in our culture (e.g., "only weak losers get in trouble with drugs", "all addicts are liars and can't be trusted"). These difficult thoughts and feelings not only result in shame, but can also push in 3 potential negative directions: a desire to isolate or withdraw from others; an effort to make up for errors by being "perfect"; or, a tendency to blame others because what you are feeling is so painful.

Isolating - At it's core, shame is full of self-judgments, and it's often accompanied by a fear that others are judging us just as harshly. This is a particularly destructive aspect of shame as it causes you to pull away from the support of others and instead move toward isolation. You may find yourself thinking everyone else seems to have their life in order (e.g., "None of my friends are dealing with this...they all seem to be fine in their relationships!") and the shame you feel causes you to keep the problem to yourself, leading to suffering alone. The shared human experience of struggle or disappointment can connect you to other people in similar situations, but shame pushes you to keep failings and setbacks to yourself.

Seeking Perfection - Another common reaction to shame is to dedicate an enormous amount of time and energy trying to accomplish the impossible – trying to avoid the future experience of shame by striving for perfection, by "making it all work." Truthfully, everyone has moments they regret, even deeply, and feel disappointed in themselves. Shame causes you to think that no one else has "screwed up" as much as you have and that you need to "make sure this never happens again." Perfection seeking, however, is the opposite of the resilience building you could use most in this struggle.

Externalizing Blame - Another common response to shame is to turn it on others: "It's THEM, not ME!" Although this distracts you from your distress in the short-term ("Can you believe what he did THIS time"!), self-doubt and self-attack lurk in the background, only to seep back in later. In addition, this reaction holds you back from taking a closer look at behaviors that may be worth changing or modifying. "Failing" and being open to looking at what is actually going wrong allows you to learn, grow, and improve. Shame causes you to keep your focus on the faults of others, preventing learning and growth on your part.

SELF-COMPASSION: AN IMPORTANT ANTIDOTE

While painful, being aware of shame can help you change the course of things for yourself and your partner. Put simply, taking the time to experience the emotional part of being human, such as the sadness of losses, and the regrets of damage done and opportunities missed, can lead you *back to other people* and to positive connections. You can apologize if you need to. You can ask for help and support from others who care about you or have gone through similar life circumstances. You can move forward and unload some of this baggage. Ultimately, these are all part of ***finding compassion for yourself***. If instead you stay stuck to the shame, dwelling on your "badness" or your family's "sickness," you are likely to be led away from other people and into hiding.

And finding compassion for yourself? Easier said than done but crucially important. Self-compassion involves noticing your suffering (e.g., becoming aware of shame, sadness, stress, anger, etc.), practicing self-kindness during painful experiences, and recognizing suffering as an aspect of life experienced by everyone. How will strengthening your self-compassion muscles benefit you? First and foremost, it contributes to the "oxygen" you need, the "fuel in the tank" to manage difficult situations with your partner. Modeling this way of relating to yourself (with kindness and care) will also help your partner learn how to deal with the pains of life in a gentler and healthier manner (they have an inner critic within them too).

But we want to be practical again. Left unattended, shame is corrosive, exhausting and harmful to everyone, not just you. And as with many things we describe in the 20 Minute Guide, it takes practice to shift away from this pull of shame. It requires that you practice treating yourself kindly during and after moments that do not go so well. It is inevitable that mistakes will be made and that you will stumble, maybe time and time again. Tripping may be beyond your control, but you *can* control how you respond to each fall, including responding to *yourself* in a kinder, gentler and more respectful manner. The truth is, however, that many people don't believe they are deserving or capable of self-kindness. Fortunately this is a skill that can be fostered and strengthened through - PRACTICE! PRACTICE! PRACTICE! It is also one you cannot afford to ignore in this guide.

SHAME AND SELF COMPASSION: WORKSHEET

Start with the exercise of trying to see the difference between "rethinking" thoughts (those that are about other ways you could have done things), and "shaming" thoughts (or those that contain accusations about your personal defects or failures that "caused" these problems).

"Rethinking/regretful" thoughts:

1. "I *wish I* had known about _____ earlier on."
2. "It's painful at holidays covering for my husband."
3. "Perhaps if I tried to do _____, then things would have turned out differently."
4. "I wish I was able to be less angry."

"Shaming" thoughts:

1. "I *should* have known about _____ earlier on."
2. Maybe we'll skip Thanksgiving… it's so humiliating dealing with these questions." (isolating)
3. "How did I not think to try _____, then things would have turned out differently." (perfectionism)
4. "My anger is totally unacceptable" (shame turned to blame)

Next, write several shaming thoughts you have had recently related to interactions, feelings or events around your partner's substance use struggles. Then, try to re-phrase that shaming thought into one that may express regret, but is not shaming of you or another.

"Shaming" thought: _____

"Rethinking/regretful" thoughts: _____

"Shaming" thought: _____

"Rethinking/regretful" thoughts: _____

"Shaming" thought: _____

"Rethinking/regretful" thoughts: _____

This practice, of noticing the shame basis of certain thoughts and then working to "re-do" them in a more self-accepting way, is a powerful step toward self-compassion and relief from the toxic effects of shame.

APPRECIATING YOU!

To start to get the important benefits of kindness and openness (as opposed to shame), it is important to practice an attitude of kindness and openness toward ourselves not only in response to our shortcomings, but our strengths as well. Just as we all have imperfections, we all have strengths. In the exercise below, take several moments to acknowledge some of the strengths you possess. List ten qualities that you really appreciate about yourself. If you get uncomfortable, remind yourself that you are not claiming that you are perfect or better than anyone else. You are simply noting the good qualities that you sometimes display.

1.	6.
2.	7.
3.	8.
4.	9.
5.	10.

CHAPTER IV

HELPING WITH WORDS

As you well know, communication breaks down in the face of stress and high emotion. Therefore, developing new communication strategies may be the most powerful thing you can do to improve your situation and help your partner. Good communication is crucial in creating space for change to take place, and it can effectively tip the motivational seesaw towards it. More than that, developing your communication skills will help you feel more understood, listened to, and better in ALL the relationships in which you practice them. You might feel tempted to jump ahead to the "Helping with Actions" section, feeling understandably anxious to see changes in your partner's behavior and start doing what you can as quickly as possible. We urge you, however, to not skip over this communication section because so many of the active strategies of CRAFT that come later truly rely on good, effective communication to have the impact you want, which is why we have purposefully put communication first in the order.

Our topics in this communication section include how to listen more effectively, how to offer feedback and information, and how to make requests most constructively, with the least amount of argumentation or defensiveness. We also discuss the importance of validation and empathy throughout communication, and how to stay out of conversational "traps." But we begin with the overarching goal: keeping a connection and sense of positive forward movement through a communication. We think of this as keeping track of whether the traffic lights (of communication) are red or green.

THIS SECTION INCLUDES FIVE TOPICS:

1. COMMUNICATE WITH LOVE: LISTENING

You've probably heard it said that love is not a noun; it's a verb. According to an acronym that helps people remember communication skills, LOVE is *four* verbs: **Listening**, **Offering**, **Validating,** and **Empathizing**.

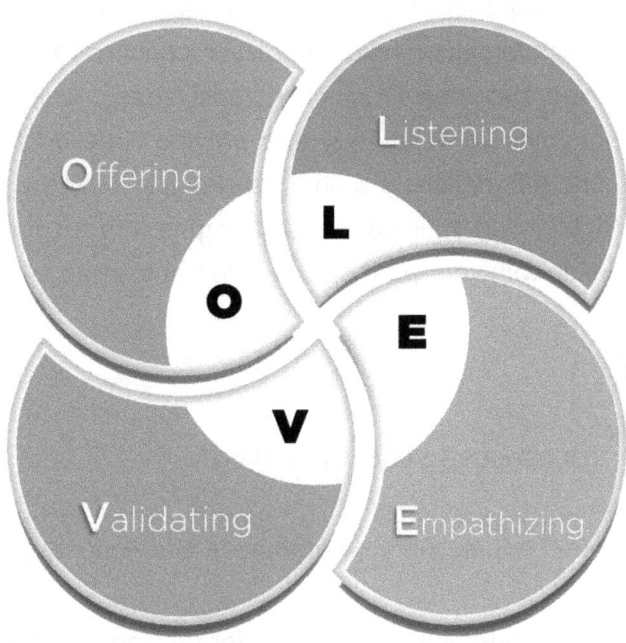

LISTENING

There are many ways to listen to another person, some more helpful than others. A powerful therapeutic approach called Motivational Interviewing emphasizes four strategies: open-ended questioning, affirming, reflecting or active listening, and summarizing. It's an approach to listening that helps the red lights turn green, instead of driving straight through and hoping things work out.

1. **Open-ended questions** – These are questions that call for some elaboration, that can't be answered with one word (e.g. *"What concerns you most?" "What would you like to be different?"*). Open questions invite description, giving you, the listener, more to listen to and learn from. They also set a collaborative tone, as they communicate more interest in your partner's view. Open-ended questions should be inviting information (from them), not suggesting information (from you).

Closed question	Open-ended question
"Don't you feel bad that your boss called you into his office?"	*"What was your reaction when your boss called you into his office?"*
"Do you wish we'd stayed later at that party?"	*"Tell me what you liked about that party?"*

2. **Affirmations** – Listen for the positives. Communication can easily become all about what's wrong. Noticing what's going right and explicitly acknowledging it can change everything: it puts some balance back in the conversation, holds a positive connection, and keeps you headed for green lights. How? Affirming statements reduce defensiveness, which helps when you get to tougher issues (what's not going so well). They also provide direction, increase self-esteem and reinforce positive behaviors. Affirmations are not cheerleading, which is more general; they refer to something specific. Highlighting your partner's strengths and recognizing positive behaviors will improve your relationship with your partner *and* help her to change.

For example, you can:

• Acknowledge effort: "It's obvious you are trying hard."

• State your appreciation: "I appreciate your openness and honesty today."

• Catch the person doing something right: "Thanks for helping my mom out today."

• Give a compliment: "I like the way you said that. You are really good with people."

• Express hope, caring, or support: "I hope this weekend goes well for you!"

3. **Reflections** – Also called **active listening**, reflections involve restating some or all of what you think the person talking to you said. Your reflection can simply restate the words you heard, or it may reflect the feeling in the words; it can even infer meaning, as long as you are open to maybe getting it wrong! Reflections are statements, not questions (which can slow down or redirect the other person).

As well as communicating that you understand what your partner is saying, reflections make sure you actually *do* understand what she is saying—or, if you get it wrong, that you are trying. Reflecting is not necessarily agreeing, but it is being willing to hear how your partner sees things, instead of immediately countering. Reflective listening helps a discussion go forward, even or especially after you've hit a red light.

4. **Summaries** – With open questions, affirmations, and reflections, you may end up in a long and productive conversation! **Summarizing** communicates that you were listening, and helps pull together the important things that were said. It can also help your partner tie his thoughts together in a way that might lead her to connect certain dots. Summaries can even guide the conversation toward a next step, without forcing an agenda. Like reflections, summaries should come with permission for your partner to disagree with or correct the record as you recount it. Try to summarize as accurately as possible, without editing the conversation to include what you wished she had said.

OPEN QUESTIONS

Start with words like *How ("How are things going?")* or *What ("What would be most helpful?")*. (Try to avoid *Why* questions, which can prompt your partner to justify her negative behaviors.) Open questions can even be a statement, as in, *"Tell me more about that..."* If a question can be answered with one word, such as "yes" or "no," it is a closed question. Closed questions make you work harder trying to find the "perfect" question, and they usually do not get you the answer you were looking for. Consider how you have phrased certain questions in the past and try to turn them into open questions.

Closed Questions	Open Questions
Did you drink last night?	How did you manage your drinking last night?
Don't you want to change?	What would be different if you changed your use of _____?
Why did you do that?	Tell me more about that...

AFFIRMATIONS

Note some ways that your partner has tried to explain her behavior in the past; then imagine affirming responses you could use that recognize the behavior you want her to continue.

Situation	Affirming Statement
I tried not to use but it didn't work out last night.	You took a stab at doing something difficult.
I know I didn't tell you until you asked me about it.	I appreciate you talking honestly to me about this now.
I DID try to at least not start drinking until later in the party...	It took some courage to try something different last night.

REFLECTIONS

Recall some things your partner has said to you about how she feels, and how you have responded in the past. Then try to reconstruct your response to make it reflective. Notice the impulse to "correct" what your partner is saying. What you get for your correction is usually further justification by her of her "rightness." What you get for letting her have her version of events is a greater likelihood that she will hear another perspective.

Your Partner's Statement	"Counter" Response	"Reflective" Response
You never listen to me.	That's not true, I...	You don't feel like I'm hearing you...
I don't want to stop drinking.	Don't you see that you have a problem?!	Alcohol is really important to you right now.
I didn't use last night.	Yeah, but it's only one night.	Not using was a priority for you last night and you were successful.

The Partner's 20 Minute Guide

THE INFORMATION SANDWICH

Information and feedback figure in any human interchange and the "information sandwich" technique is a three-step process for making information (the contents of the sandwich) palatable for the other person. By layering information between asking permission and checking back or clarifying afterwards, sandwiching helps the person receive it, take it in, and feel empowered to use it.

1. **Asking permission** – This conversational equivalent of knocking on the door before you enter has several benefits. First, by asking permission to give them information, you help the other person make a fundamental motivational shift: you allow him to invite you in. Consider your own interactions: if someone shows up at your house unexpectedly, it's a different proposition than when you have asked for the company. In the latter case, you can prepare and arrange things in a way that is comfortable for you. You can give your partner a similar courtesy in conversation.

For example:

- *"Would it be helpful for you to hear about…?"*

- *"Could I offer a thought?"*

- *"Can I ask a question?"*

- *"I have a couple of ideas…but did you want to say your ideas first?"*

- *"Is it alright if I express one concern I have about this plan?"*

Asking permission is one way to make sure the light is green *before* you proceed with the content of your discussion, and it increases the chances that the light *will* be green, as it enhances your partner's sense of safety and control. Plus, it honors his autonomy by giving him a choice. This may seem like a small point, but it can have a profound effect on the conversation when your partner feels like he is a participant rather than a passive or reluctant recipient of your words—the difference between talking *at* and talking *with*. This spirit of collaboration is fundamental to motivational therapies and is equally powerful in conversations. Asking permission increases the likelihood that the other person will hear what follows. One last point: truly asking permission means leaving room for them to say "No, I'd rather not hear this right now." It is **so** much better to know this than to speak to deaf ears.

2. **Providing information** – Permission granted, you would relate the information or feedback in question. Here are a few tips.

- *Provide options.* Whenever possible, it helps to offer more than one good option. It's harder to reject multiple options wholesale, as it puts your partner in a position to weigh the pros and cons of each rather than simply say "no."

- *Offer; don't impose.* By the same logic of asking permission, your partner will more likely hear, appreciate, and use information that is offered rather than forced on him.

- *Allow disagreement.* As much as possible, leave room for your partner to not accept or agree with the information. By asking permission and providing options you better the chances that he will, but it's still his right to disagree. Collaborators don't tell each other what to do; they resolve it together. Allowing for disagreement means the conversation doesn't depend on agreement to go forward or, conversely, come to a screeching halt every time you disagree.

Reflecting your partner's autonomy will help you stay in communication and encounter less defensiveness—in other words, more green lights.

3. **Checking back or clarifying** – The top layer of the sandwich helps your partner process the information and remain open to the discussion. Essentially, you want to know how the information was received: whether your partner understood the information or feedback, whether it was digestible or emotionally acceptable—or did he get too mad, hurt, or sad to take in what you said?—and so on. For example:

- "Does that make sense to you?"

- "I just wanted to check back about…"

- "I'm not sure I said that very clearly…"

All together, the sandwich technique is a great way to keep communication open and constructive, offering chances to understand if there is a breakdown, as well as to develop collaboration.

OFFERING INFORMATION WORKSHEET

Think of a circumstance in which you have information or feedback to give—to your partner or to another person in your life—about substance use or anything else. This exercise will show you how to build an information sandwich around it. Start with the middle, information layer, and consider how the other person might react. Next, write out how you will ask for permission first, and how you will check back after. Then consider how the other person's experience of the information, and his reaction to it, might differ given the sandwich.

Step 1: Write down the information or feedback you would like to give to another person.

I would like to let _____ [person's name] know that:

_____.

Step 2: What kind of reaction do you imagine?

_____.

Step 3: Now put the content from Step 1 in a "sandwich":

How will you ask for permission to give them this information?

_____.

How will you check back?

_____.

Step 4: Consider how this interaction might go differently (versus Step 1 alone) using the permission sandwich.

_____.

Remember, you can practice any new skill in lower risk, less difficult situations and relationships first. Then, when you're ready, try it with your partner in testier circumstances and see how it goes.

3. COMMUNICATE WITH LOVE: VALIDATING AND EMPATHIZING

The last two letters of LOVE have less to do with specific strategies and more with the background music of communication: understanding where your partner is coming from, or what it's like to walk the world in her shoes (empathy); and acknowledging her experience—her thoughts, feelings, motivations, and perspective—as valid (validation). As we discussed with the use of reflections, you can validate and empathize without endorsing your partner's behavior.

VALIDATING

Validating is the simple act of acknowledging another person's experience without needing to qualify it in any way. People who are struggling with substance use often assume that others judge and will critique their behaviors without understanding what might motivate those behaviors. They can end up with a pervasive sense of feeling invalidated by everyone around them, which understandably decreases self-esteem and increases defensiveness. Assuring your partner that you do not view her as stupid or crazy takes a major tinderbox out of the conversation.

EMPATHIZING

Also not a strategy, but a powerful function of communication, empathy is truly feeling "where the other person is coming from"—how she understands her situation, her point of view—and conveying this in some way to your partner, often in only a few words ("wow, that seems really nerve-wracking"; "that would have upset me too"). It is a powerful tool in reducing shame and helping your partner open up to different ways of thinking about things.

Both empathizing and validating are conveyed through your attitude and approach (respectful, kind, open, and so on) as much as with specific words.

Together, these four aspects of communicating with L-O-V-E will facilitate hearing, being heard, and communicating in a more caring, respectful way with your partner as well as in your life. We again suggest practicing as the key to getting better at these skills, and in particular practicing in "easier," less stressful situations, rather than starting with the most important and tension-filled topic you need to discuss with your partner.

4. THE 7 ELEMENTS OF POSITIVE COMMUNICATION

In addition to the LOVE communication skills taken from Motivational Interviewing, CRAFT prescribes **positive communication skills** as additional communication strategies for your toolbox. You might be thinking: "wouldn't that be nice…to just be positive!" But CRAFT breaks it down into seven elements, all within your reach. These elements will improve any kind of communication, but they are especially useful for *making requests*. What we have found with these seven elements is they are both straightforward *and* difficult to do, so practice is important.

"Positive communication" does not mean only saying nice things and avoiding conflict. Here's what it does mean: (For examples and more explanation, see our chapter on Positive Communication in *Beyond Addiction*.)

1
Be Brief

Most people say more than necessary when they haven't planned it in advance, especially when nervous or angry. Try to hone in on your central request ahead of time, and stick to it. Script, edit, and rehearse what you want to say as concisely as possible. Extraneous words can drown out your core message (as in the "waa waa waa" of Charlie Brown's teacher).

2
Be Specific

Vague requests are easy to ignore or misunderstand, and are often difficult to translate into concrete behavior. In contrast, referring to specific behaviors instead of thoughts or feelings makes change observable, measurable, and reinforceable. For instance, instead of telling your partner to "be more responsible," specify a behavior you want to see more of: "I'd really appreciate it if you called me in the afternoon if you will be late coming home from work."

3
Be Positive

Where "positive" entails describing what you want, instead of what you don't want. This shifts the framing from critical and complaining to supportive and doable, and ties into positive reinforcement strategies, since it's easier to reward someone for doing something—a concrete, verifiable thing—than for not doing something. Being positive in this way decreases defensiveness and promotes motivation. Framed positively, "Stop making a mess in the kitchen" becomes "Please put your dishes in the sink when you're done."

4
Label Your Feelings

Kept brief and in proportion, a description of your emotional reaction to the problem at hand can help elicit empathy and consideration from your partner. For best results, state your feelings in a calm, nonaccusatory manner. If your feelings are very intense it can be good strategy to tone them down, so if you were feeling "furious and terrified" you might say "frustrated and worried."

5
Offer An Understanding Statement

The more the other person believes that you "get" why he is acting the way he is, the less defensive he will be and the more likely to hear you and oblige. Plus, trying to understand your partner's perspective builds your empathy, which will help the relationship.

6
Take Partial Responsibility

Sharing in a problem, even a tiny piece of the problem, decreases defensiveness and promotes collaboration. It shows your partner that you're interested in solving, not blaming. Accepting partial responsibility does not mean taking the blame or admitting fault; it communicates "We're in this together."

7
Offer to Help

Especially when phrased as a question, an offer to help can communicate non-blaming, problem-solving support. Try asking, "Would it help if . . . ?" Or simply, "How can I help?" A little goes a long way to improve communication and generate ideas. ("Yeah, if you texted me a reminder, that would help.")

---

*   Adapted from pp.111-115 in: Smith, J., & Myers, R. (2004). Motivating substance abusers to enter treatment: working with family members. New York: Guilford Press.

              The Partner's 20 Minute Guide

POSITIVE COMMUNICATION WORKSHEET

Don't expect fully formed positive communications to spring from your lips spontaneously. Like any new skill, it will probably feel awkward at first. Start by writing down what you want to say. Rehearse, fine-tune, role-play with someone else to see how it goes before you go live. Use this exercise to plan a request you would like to make of your partner.

Step 1:
Write out your request, as you'd usually say it.

_____

_____

_____

_____

Step 2:
Now modify your request according to the seven elements of positive communication.

Be Brief. Only one request at a time, and stick to your point. (No: "and another thing…!")

First Try:	Modified:
You need to do a better job coming home on time. You are stopping at the bar first and it's driving me crazy.	I would like you to have dinner with us.

Your brief, positive request:

_____

_____

_____

_____

Be Specific. Make sure you are clear about your request.

First Try:	Modified:
It would be nice if you cared.	*Coming home on time would really help me with the kids.*

Your specific, brief, positive request:

_____

_____

_____

_____

_____

_____

Be Positive. Tell your partner what you want him to do rather than what you *don't* want him to do.

First Try:	Modified:
Stop coming home so late.	*Please come home in time for dinner.*

Your positive request:

_____

_____

_____

_____

_____

Label your feelings. Identify a feeling and describe it without being too intense or lengthy. Bonus points for also including a positive feeling.

First Try:	Modified:
It makes me crazy how little you seem to care about things!	I feel frustrated when you stop at the bar first. I'd really appreciate your help with dinner.

Your feeling(s) labeled:

_____

_____

_____

_____

_____

Offer an understanding statement. Use this strategy to help your partner feel heard and non-defensive.

First Try:	Modified:
I'm not asking anything of you that I don't ask of everyone else in this house.	I know you feel stressed after work and think a drink will help you unwind.

Your understanding statement:

_____

_____

_____

_____

_____

Take partial responsibility. This is not saying it's your fault, but it's helpful to find a piece of the problem, however small, that you can share.

First Try:	Modified:
I have a job too and it's not my job to take care of everyone!	I realize I haven't told you how much it bothers me. I can't expect you to read my mind!

Your acceptance of partial responsibility:

_____

_____

_____

_____

Offer to help. See if there is anything you can do to help your partner achieve your request.

First Try:	Modified:
I can't do everything around here!	Would it help to have a few minutes before dinner to unwind?

Your offer to help:

_____

_____

_____

_____

_____

Now try putting it all together. You can play with the order and wording to make it sound as natural as possible. Keep in mind that even the most perfectly scripted request won't guarantee the outcome you want. It will, however, increase the odds of being heard.

TIPS FOR PRACTICE:

1. Start with small-ticket items that are less important; also start by practicing in the context of safer or easier relationships (practice with a friend or sister instead of your partner).

2. You don't need to use all seven steps in every interaction. (Though trying all of them, at least for practice, can help you get the hang of it.)

3. Watch the timing of when you deliver your request. It should not be when your partner is under the influence or hung over, and you both should be in reasonably good moods and not rushing off somewhere.

4. Try not to get discouraged if it doesn't go so well the first few or many times. It takes effort and practice to get out of negative ruts. We believe—because research shows—it's worth it.

There are classic communication traps you can recognize a mile away…if you know what to look for. Here are some of the most common.

The Information Trap: *If only he knew the facts he would see things differently and change.* Information can be helpful, especially when it fills a gap. It is less helpful to tell your partner something he already knows. When you do have fresh information, offering it in a "sandwich" (as you learned in Section 3), will maximize the chances that it gets across. But there are no magic words for change, so try to be patient. Improving the quality of your communication over time will help, as well as being a valuable change in and of itself.

The Lecture Trap: This is a deeper information trap. One sign that you have entered this trap is when you find yourself talking "at" your partner about what you think he should do, what his problems are, what went wrong last week, and so on, rather than talking "with" him.

The Labeling Trap: Labels are not necessary for change, and at times get in the way. This trap results in a conversation being about labels and not behavior. ("You're an addict." —"No, I'm not.")

The Blaming Trap: When you're worried, frustrated, or sad about a situation, it is easy to get stuck in the blaming trap—who is at fault or who is to blame? This trap shuts down a conversation and backs your partner's motivation into a corner.

The Taking-Sides Trap: If you take only one side of a discussion, it's practically a set up for your partner to take the other, and she may end up defending behaviors she actually feels ambivalent about. Instead of one side against the other you can be on the same side, the side of constructive conversation, considering different options together.

The Question-and-Answer Trap: <u>Closed questions</u> set off this trap and result in an interview, or worse, an interrogation ("Did you get high last night? Did you forget your phone? Did you do the errand you said you would?"). Open questions are more likely to steer your conversation to a productive exchange.

CHAPTER V

HELPING WITH ACTIONS

This section will cover a variety of critical tools for encouraging change in your partner's behavior and motivation. It follows "Helping with Self Care" and "Helping with Words" because the skills in those sections are the foundations of sustaining change and keeping things on track day-to-day. The tools in this section will help you understand motivation and how it is different for different people, how to reinforce new and positive behaviors as well as how to deal with negative behaviors, how to understand and allow for ambivalence in your partner (and the sometimes jagged upward course of change), and very importantly, paying attention to collaboration with other people who care about your partner.

THIS SECTION INCLUDES FIVE TOPICS:

1 How to Solve a Problem

2 Community Support Network Collaboration
Community Support Network Collaboration Worksheet

3 Reinforcement: Your Love Matters
Reinforcement Worksheet

4 Natural Consequences: Allowing Them to Happen
Natural Consequences Worksheet

5 Your Consequences: Making Them Happen
Your Consequences Worksheet

The Partner's 20 Minute Guide

1. HOW TO SOLVE A PROBLEM

We start with the topic of problem solving because that's what you are facing! Your partner's substance use, as well as the ensuing problems with communication, behavior, co-parenting, socializing, and work performance (you name it!). We will discuss all of these issues in depth, but as we start this process we want you to have a general strategy for approaching ANY problem.

CRAFT (among other behavioral approaches) sets out seven steps for solving problems.* This approach will take you beyond painful avoidance strategies and unreliable quick fixes, to help you work through problems thoroughly and systematically. As you practice with these steps, try to apply (and give yourself credit for) what you already do well, and take the time you need to learn what would be useful that you don't already know.

1

Define the problem as narrowly as you can.

Often what people take as "the problem" is actually many smaller problems lumped together. No wonder they feel overwhelmed. When you describe a problem, be on the lookout for multiple problems embedded within your description, and tease them apart. The idea is to tackle one relatively discrete problem at a time. Solutions are more manageable with a series of smaller problems and you'll feel more accomplished and optimistic as you get through each one.

2

Brainstorm possible solutions.

In this step, your task is to write down as many solutions as you can think of, to foster a sense of possibility and give yourself some choice. Brainstorming is an open, free-for-all process of allowing every idea in the door as they come, to be sorted and refined later. Your inner critic will tend to dismiss ideas out of habit or fear; but some of these could be viable options if you gave them a chance. List without judging. Try not to rule out anything before you've written down every conceivable solution to your problem.

3

Eliminate unwanted ideas.

Now that you have an exhaustive list of potential solutions, you can examine them more closely and cross out any that are unappealing. Eliminate options that you can't actually imagine ever doing, have too many downsides, or seem unrealistic. If you end up crossing off every idea, then return to step 2 and brainstorm again.

4

Select one potential solution or goal.

Pick one solution that seems doable to you, that you can see yourself trying this week. Hint: a doable goal is put in brief, simple, and positive terms (what you will do, not what you won't do or haven't been doing), is specific and measurable, reasonable and achievable, in your control, and involves skills you already have or are learning. (For a detailed discussion of goal setting, see Chapter 8 of our book, *Beyond Addiction*.)

5

Identify possible obstacles.

Next, identify potential obstacles that could get in the way of completing your task. By anticipating problems you can plan strategies for dealing with them. This can include specific, predictable obstacles as well as a more general awareness that unforeseen challenges may arise, which can lend you some emotional resilience in dealing with them.

6

Address each obstacle.

Design specific strategies to cope with each obstacle. Not just, "I'm sure I can deal with it," but exactly how you will get past it and move forward.

7

See how things go.

After you've carried out your plan, evaluate the process... How did it go? Look at what went well and what was more challenging in the implementation. Did your strategies for dealing with obstacles work well? Did obstacles come up that you hadn't predicted? Is there anything you would do differently next time? This is how you figure out what works and what doesn't work for you.

---

*   Adapted from pp.187-190 in: Smith, J., & Myers, R. (2004). Motivating substance abusers to enter treatment: working with family members. New York: Guilford Press.

2. COMMUNITY SUPPORT
NETWORK COLLABORATION

Often, when someone is struggling with substance use or other compulsive behavior problems, communication breaks down *among the people who love that person*. Most people struggle to not get defensive or lose their cool in situations they don't understand or know how to control. And when a loved one is doing risky, upsetting things, it's not uncommon for people to either feel at wits' end *with each other*, or to disengage completely from each other. Disagreements are understandable. After all, wives and mother-in-laws (for example) are not always aligned in their goals or perspectives of their husband/son in the best of circumstances; the more serious the issue, the more polarizing it can be. But helping can be significantly aided by finding ways to collaborate with the other adults in your life who have an influence and love the person with the problem.

As you try to help your partner change their relationship with substances, it will be easier if others in your life are also giving clear and consistent feedback and reinforcing positive behaviors. If you could magically transform all the people who use substances with your partner into people who do healthy activities with her, it would be ideal! You're not likely to achieve that goal, but it's worth considering who might be receptive to playing even a small helping role. Change, even change for the better, is difficult and your partner will likely feel ambivalent about it. It will be hard for her to change who she spends time with and what they do together. The more ambivalent she is, the more important it is for as many people in her social world to respond with consistent support of her changes. For instance, if your brother-in-law smokes marijuana with your wife, this will undermine her process of positive change.

Additionally, the more support you feel from other adults in your life, the less stressed and alone you will feel. And with less conflict and stress in general you can, in turn, be more positive with your partner.

Collaboration with other adults in your lives doesn't mean across-the-board, united-front agreement on "the party line." Nor does it mean you should go about exposing your partner's struggles. Your partner would likely feel infantilized if everyone suddenly changed how they treated him or if he felt you were getting people to "gang up" on him. However, if slowly but surely, others who love him started making efforts to invite him to non-using activities, and when concerned individuals started communicating with him using the same strategies you are learning (at the very least working on positive communication as opposed to confrontation or overt anger and frustration), could provide a wonderful community support for his positive changes.

We suggest three guidelines when considering getting support from your community network. First, it is important to think through who can actually be a consistent positive support, instead of trying to enlist everyone who may be closely involved in their life to somehow "apply pressure." Some people in the "inner circle" are not really up to the task of being a positive support for any number of reasons. The important point is not that they SHOULD be part of a collaborative team, but that YOU try to recognize who can be most helpful, and know that this doesn't have to include everyone.

Second, as in the seven steps of positive communication we discussed earlier, it can be helpful to think of the positive actions that could be taken with community support, as opposed to the negative events you are trying to avoid. That is, your partner is more likely to benefit from invitations to healthy activities, instead of you spending time working on making sure he is not invited to potentially negative or triggering activities, which often just results in feeling excluded or punished.

Last, it is quite useful to try to reduce second-hand communication, and have direct feedback between people. Your partner is more likely to be receptive to hearing feedback directly from others about their observations and feelings, rather than hearing you describe what others have told you or what you think others have observed.

Brainstorm about situations with other concerned adults in your life. Which of those people might be receptive to supporting your partner's process of change? How, specifically, might particular people be able to help from their unique perspectives? Start small, and try to manage your expectations... set doable goals in how you will communicate and honestly weigh the pros and cons of saying anything at all.

Step 1: Brainstorm ways you can respond the next time someone expresses concern about your partner's behaviors. Don't rule out any ideas at first glance, even if you are not ready to try them yet. Consider the pros and cons of each idea, and see if you'd be willing to try it. When you've chosen one, use the positive communication worksheet to practice how you'll say it using the 7 communication steps. And then practice!

<u>Communication idea</u>: *My husband's father pours him a stiff drink as soon as we arrive for a visit but complains under his breath at the end of the night when my husband is drunk. I could find a way to elicit his thoughts about my husband's drinking and feel out his receptivity to doing something (e.g. that first drink-offer) differently.*

<u>Pros</u>:	<u>Cons</u>:
1. *My husband might drink less during these visits.*	1. *It might have no effect on my husband's drinking and I'll feel worse.*
2. *I won't dread visiting my in-laws.*	2. *My father-in-law might not speak with me about this because he's ashamed/too proud/ etc.*
3. *I might feel closer and supported by my in-laws.*	3. *My husband might feel betrayed if he finds out I said anything at all.*

Communication idea: *At parties when my wife is using, often one of our friends will give me a knowing glance (which we all understand to be about her cocaine use) and ask how I'm coping. Instead of pretending nothing's wrong, I could find a way to respond that encourages them to speak with my wife directly about their concerns. Or I could ask them to have lunch or coffee sometime for my own support.*

Pros:	Cons:
1. *I will feel more supported by people I know care.*	1. *I might feel ashamed to discuss these problems in more detail.*
2. *I might get some new good ideas from a fresh perspective.*	2. *I might feel stressed by taking time out for lunch.*
3. *My wife might be more impacted to hear one of our friends directly express concern.*	3. *My wife might blame me for whatever the friend says.*

Your communication idea:

_____

_____

_____

Pros:	Cons:

Step 2: Go back to the positive communication steps and craft a message using the 7 steps for communicating in one of your identified situations.

_____

_____

_____

Step 3: When you have selected the situation, the person, and the communication, list potential obstacles that come to mind. Then, think of coping skills you could use to maximize your chances of getting around each obstacle and reaching your goal(s).

Obstacle	Coping Skill
I might lose my nerve in the moment.	I will make a point of getting back in touch with that friend the following day to say what I'd planned.
I might feel too nervous about one of the "cons" on my list.	I will re-do my communication to see if there's a way to discuss it that will decrease these concerns.

3. REINFORCEMENT: YOUR LOVE MATTERS

Since you now know that "your partner's behavior makes sense" because substance use is reinforcing, we can move on to positive reinforcement as one of the core helping strategies in CRAFT. That is, you can use the same behavioral mechanisms that reinforce substance use to reinforce other behaviors instead. Basically, reward your partner when she does something that you want her to do again (coming home sober, doing the errands, talking in a calm manner, being helpful to other family members). A reward can be a compliment, a hug, a favorite meal, or—and this is often overlooked—simply acknowledging what she has done. Linked to a behavior, such positive recognition helps your partner start to see the value in acting that way again. Your part is to figure out what's rewarding to her and tolerate the discomfort you may feel in rewarding behavior you think she "should be doing anyway."

Is reinforcement bribery?

How will your partner learn to want change herself if she is "just" doing it for the reward?

In fact, positive reinforcement, when practiced consistently, helps your partner's internal motivation. Why? Because with practice, over time, she will experience the benefits of the new behavior and it will become rewarding in and of itself. Meanwhile, your reinforcement boosts her willingness to engage in new behaviors in the first place, so that she can start experiencing the intrinsic benefits of positive change.

HOW WILL REINFORCING CHANGE ANYTHING?

The value in reinforcing positive behavior by rewarding it is that it can start to compete with the reinforcing effects of drugs and alcohol. In essence, your partner can learn to "feel good" in other ways rather than using substances. They can feel proud of themselves, acknowledged, recognized for their efforts—all the feel good things that contribute to a healthy self-esteem and ability to cope with life.

WHAT MIGHT BE HAPPENING INSTEAD

Contrary to what you might have heard, confrontation and punishment are not the most helpful strategies to use when you are trying to encourage change. In fact, they are likely to push things in the exact opposite direction as your partner acts to defend his position. Detaching is not the answer either, because it leaves you with no way to positively influence your partner. It may also be that your partner's *un*healthy behavior gets most if not all of your attention, even at times when she isn't using—because you're still fuming after the last time, or worried about the next. When a family is caught in a cycle of confrontation and punishment, negative attention may be the only kind of attention your partner receives.

While your negative feelings are understandable, they can prevent you from noticing the good things that also happen (when she's sober and helping the kids with homework, sober and having dinner with the family, and so on). It may seem to your partner that she can't do anything right (because you are upset all the time), so why bother? The key to your partner making changes that stick will be your attention (which is a reward in and of itself) to the healthy, adaptive behaviors that you see. Reward your partner when she is not using! In other words, "catch her being good" (as rare as that may seem sometimes!). Staying involved and rewarding steps towards healthy behavior is what will work to help motivate your partner.

Take a moment to think about meaningful rewards for your partner. Here are a few guidelines:

- **Rewards are in the eye of the beholder.**
  A 2-hour massage might feel like winning the lottery to you, but for your partner, going skydiving or taking surfing lessons might hit closer to the mark. Spend some time thinking by yourself or talking to your partner about what she finds rewarding. You can also look around for what rewards she is already getting that you might want to tie to her behavior.

- **Find rewards that fit your partner's needs in her current stage of dealing with substance use.**
  For example, if your partner has been working at changing her substance use for some time and is committed to it, verbally acknowledging her efforts might feel like a lovely reward to her; however if she doesn't even see drinking as a problem yet, linking a "reward" of flowers or time together to her not drinking might serve to make her feel infantilized.

- **Have the rewards follow closely the behavior they're meant to reward.**
  Timing helps link the reward to the behavior, so plan rewards that you can deliver immediately or shortly after (not before) the behavior takes place. Resist the temptation to give something now in the hopes that her behavior will change later.

- **Make sure the rewards are things you're willing and able to give.**
  Make sure you're comfortable with the cost and other qualities of the rewards you choose. A new motorcycle might be something she'd really like, but if it's not compatible with your values and budget, think of something else. Some of the most effective rewards, like your attention, compliments, and affection, are free.

For more guidelines and examples of reinforcement in action, see our whole chapter about it in *Beyond Addiction*.

Practiced consistently over time, positive reinforcement will enhance your partner's motivation to change. Try to have patience and don't give up if her behavior doesn't change as fast as you'd like it to. Change takes time. If you're uncertain or find yourself thinking "this doesn't work for my partner" or "he doesn't care about anything", review the guidelines: Is the reward rewarding to your partner? How's your timing? And bear in mind, consistent behavior change is hard for everyone. Try to tolerate the process and remember that changing behavior patterns takes willingness to resist engaging in them long enough to learn new ones. It's a lot of work!

The Partner's 20 Minute Guide

REINFORCEMENT: WORKSHEET

Reinforcement requires noticing when your partner is sober and doing something you like, and rewarding it. This not only increases the likelihood that she'll repeat the desired behavior, it also contributes to a general sense that her world when she's sober is more rewarding than her world when she's using.

Note: It is NOT reinforcing if you give rewards BEFORE the behavior happens…so resist the temptation to give something NOW in the hopes that their behavior will change LATER.

Step 1: List behaviors you hope will change, and identify a specific, alternative, healthy behavior you would be willing to support for each of them.

Behavior to Change	Alternative Behavior to Reinforce
Coming home after work late and drunk.	Coming home on time and sober.
Getting up late and making the morning stressful for everyone.	Getting up on time.

Example: The behavior I will reward this week:

Coming home from work on time. It's a step towards other behaviors like coming home sober.

The behavior I will reward this week:

Step 2: Brainstorm possible rewards for the healthy behavior. Make sure some of them are free.

Free Rewards	Rewards that Cost Something
If he comes home on time, I will compliment his effort to come home instead of drinking with friends/ colleagues.	If he comes home on time I will give him a small card of appreciation.
I will rub his shoulders for a couple minutes before starting the evening routine.	If he comes home on time 5 days in a row, I will go on a hike with him Saturday morning (which he keeps asking me to do).

The rewards I will give *after* she does the behavior I want to see:

1.

2.

3.

4. NATURAL CONSEQUENCES: ALLOWING THEM TO HAPPEN

The power of positive reinforcement for positive behavior - finding ways to acknowledge your partner's moves in the right direction - is made all the more effective by how you address your partner's negative behaviors. The bottom line? Let the negative consequences resulting from "negative" behavior be felt and heard. It may surprise you to learn that the direct, negative outcomes of your partner's actions (late to work, missed social events, a cold supper)—what we call "natural consequences"—are among the most powerful promoters of change.

In many relationships, people have a variety of unspoken ways of punishing each other for negative behavior (scoffing, eye-rolling, cold-shoulder, punishing tone or yelling), but find it difficult to let actual natural consequences happen. You want to protect your partner from the effects of missing work, embarrassing himself in public or sleeping late – in part, of course, because it may impact *you* (and/or your whole family) negatively as well. From a behavioral standpoint, however, when you shield your partner from the uncomfortable result of his actions, he learns that there's no downside. The net result? Why *wouldn't* he continue the negative behaviors?

Of course, some consequences are too harmful to allow. You have to identify the negative consequences you can tolerate and let them "speak for themselves"; they will often be more convincing than anything you could say or do, and you will be relieved of the burden of arguing. The world is a powerful teacher if we let it be.

The combination of reinforcing positive behaviors and allowing the natural consequences of negative behaviors is more powerful than either strategy alone. With this "reinforcement," your partner will experience for himself the connection between positive behavior and good things happening, and start to recognize his role as the producer of good (or bad) things in his life.

WHAT IS "ENABLING"?

It's important to understand this often misused word. It means softening or removing the negative consequences of another person's negative behavior, which in effect *encourages* the continuation of that behavior. If you rush to get your partner out of bed for his brunch plans with friends, even though he stayed out too late the night before, he never has to face his upset friends. He never has to link his behavioral choice (staying out too late) with the natural consequence (upset friends). He only has to face your upset and stress, which are likely very common and easily tuned out.

The confusion? Many people think enabling means doing *anything* nice for a loved one who is abusing substances. If, in your anger and disappointment at certain negative behaviors (using drugs, coming home late), you withdraw *all* your positive attention (even when he is sober and trying to engage in a nice conversation), you create a negative environment that is not good for anyone, you or your partner. Making a difference requires understanding the difference:

Promote positive behaviors with positive outcomes.

Allow negative behaviors to have negative outcomes.

Simple, but hard to do. Keep practicing; you'll get better at it, and so will your partner.

NATURAL CONSEQUENCES: WORKSHEET

This exercise will help you identify specific negative consequences of your partner's substance use, the ways you may be intervening to protect him from them, and ways you could allow them to happen.

Step 1: What are the potential or actual natural consequences of your partner's substance use? Focus on the "safe to allow" consequences.	**Step 2**: Is there anything buffering his direct experience of these consequences? Is there anything *you* are doing, inadvertently or purposefully, to soften these downsides?	**Step 3**: What can you do to let your partner experience one or more natural consequences more directly (without putting him at too much risk)?
Coming late or missing social engagements because he is intoxicated or oversleeping.	Pestering him until he gets up and sometimes making excuses for why he won't come/will be late.	Let him miss things or face his friends directly if late.
Getting drunk at a party and inconveniencing the host by staying overnight.	Going to pick him up wherever he is or calling her a taxi.	Let him experience the embarrassment of inconveniencing the host without intervening.
Coming home late and missing dinner.	Cooking him a late dinner so he isn't hungry.	Let him figure out what to eat on his own.

The Partner's 20 Minute Guide

5. YOUR CONSEQUENCES: MAKING THEM HAPPEN

There are times when you need or want to *provide* a negative consequence for unwanted behavior. At these times, clarity and consistency are the keys.

<u>Tip</u>:

Do not use your "biggest hammer" right away. The consequence should fit the behavior, and there should be room for improvement—if you kick him out of the house at the first sign of negative behavior, you won't know whether smaller consequences (coupled with rewards for positive behavior, of course) could have influenced change.

Save the big consequences for the really big stuff, and have some smaller consequences for smaller issues. Even more important, don't threaten any consequence unless you are willing to implement it (don't threaten to kick them out unless you are ready to change your locks).

Clarity – You may want to let your partner know beforehand what will happen if she engages in the behavior you want her to avoid. This means being clear yourself: figuring out ahead of time realistic and meaningful consequences for the range of behaviors you want to address. (The consequence should match the severity of the behavior, and it must be possible and practical to enforce.) Communicating the plan in advance puts the choice in your partner's hands—she knows, going in, the consequences of acting one way versus another.

Consistency – Pick consequences you can be consistent with over time. For example, if you plan to leave a party when your partner gets intoxicated, make sure you feel relatively confident you'll have a way to leave and be able to follow through with the plan. If you think you might waver in following through, then brainstorm about how to overcome the obstacles and stay consistent.

Through planning ahead you'll be able to work around obstacles ahead of time. This will help enormously with your consistency. And consistency helps your sense of control and your partner's motivation.

<u>Note</u>: It's better not to have any consequences or rewards at all than to promise them to your partner and then not follow through. Failing to be consistent hurts your credibility as well as your ability to influence positive change for your partner.

The Partner's 20 Minute Guide

YOUR CONSEQUENCES: WORKSHEET

This worksheet is designed to help you establish a consequence for negative behavior as clearly and consistently as possible.

Step 1: In the left-hand column, list the positive versions of what you hope for in your partner's behavior. Then in the right-hand column, describe the consequence that will result from going against this behavior.

Positive Behavior	Consequence for not achieving the behavior
She will not drink at the party.	If she becomes intoxicated, I will leave without a big discussion, as planned.
She will come home for dinner abstinent.	I will excuse myself from eating with her.

Step 2: Choose one of the above, and plan how you will communicate (in advance) your expectation and consequence to your partner. Use your new communication skills.

Example: *I know it is hard sometimes to keep from drinking at parties, but I'm not comfortable staying if you become intoxicated. So I plan to leave if you're drinking, but looking forward to staying with you if you're abstinent. I'm happy to help by making sure you always have a non-alcoholic drink in your hand if you'd like?*

Your communication:

_____

_____

_____

_____

Step 3: Anticipate any obstacle(s) that might get in the way of consistently following through, and plan how you will deal with it.

Example: *I sometimes worry she can't even make her way home when she's in that state. So when I leave I will let the host know I have to leave and mention she'll need a taxi or ride home so someone else knows to keep an eye out.*

Your obstacle(s) and solution(s):

_____

_____

_____

_____

_____

CHAPTER VI

ADDITIONAL RESOURCES

Thank you for taking the time to read the 20 Minute Guide. We hope that you found it helpful in thinking through ways to help your partner, your family, and yourself! And mostly, we'd like to recognize the dedication, love and caring you have shown by spending the time and energy to try to help in these ways. If you are like many of the people we work with, we know you probably picked up the Guide under the assumption that you'd be happy only when your partner got into treatment, or stopped smoking pot, or abstained from everything. After reading the Guide however, we hope you have created a little room for the idea that change takes time, can be a work in progress, and that you and your partner can reap some benefits of change even when it is not complete.

Here are some of the concepts we hope you hang onto and refer back to as you keep trying to cultivate change in your household:

First, motivation matters a lot! And you can have an impact on your partner's motivation to change. Giving your partner only one option, not helping them find a path to change, giving them reasons to change that make sense to YOU but maybe not to them, and not understanding where they are coming from (i.e., "you're crazy for using so much!") are ALL understandable reactions. They ALL however have been shown to push things in exactly the opposite direction from what you likely want to see in your partner. In fact, they can cause your partner to move AWAY from change and often times cause them to get MORE attached to precisely the thing you hope they will give up… drugs and alcohol.

Second, using substances is a motivated behavior with an expected outcome… like reducing anxiety or depression, feeling more comfortable socially, being part of a community (what we as psychologists call "reinforcement"). In other words, people don't use substances because they are defective or wanting to provoke you, but because it GIVES them something. Understanding this helps you in several ways:

- It allows you to take the substance use less personally.

- It lets you start to think through how else some of these needs could be met without substances.

- It helps you understand ambivalence. When something is working or is reinforcing in some way, people--in this case your partner--are reluctant or at least ambivalent about giving it up.

- It helps you understand that this struggle is very different for each person and each relationship. Your partner drinks, smokes or injects for reasons that might be similar or very different than other people you know or hear about.

Third, there are specific tools you can learn and start to use that move things in the right direction:

- How you communicate. Learning to communicate positively, respectfully and collaboratively takes practice but starts to change the whole atmosphere of your household or relationship.

- What you pay attention to...like starting to notice the positive actions of your partner. This is the idea of "catch em being good," or rewarding the good stuff and not over-focusing on what is going badly helps people decide to change.

- Letting your partner learn from their mistakes...called "allowing natural consequences" in the CRAFT approach. Don't soften all the negative outcomes of their choice to use substances, instead, let the world be their teacher. Don't make YOURSELF the negative consequence...with your lectures, mood or worry. The world is a good teacher if you let it be!

Finally, taking care of yourself through all this is critical. It can't be an afterthought! The old airplane analogy of using the oxygen first so you can help others applies here… big time! Helping a partner and the family around them navigate substance problems is not typically a short term sprint, and is sometimes a marathon. You need to take care of yourself regularly and methodically to keep the tank fueled up and functioning well if you are going to be there at the finish line. You'll always want to go that extra mile no matter what, when no one else would. We want you to respect and care for that compassion and energy you bring --it's your most valuable resource.

We hope you take the time to sit for 20-minutes a day to think about how you can use these concepts. Taking a little time every day to think through things you can change through the strategies suggested will help you have a positive effect on your partner. We know this is hard; we hope you find the support you need to persevere, and that you and your family can begin to thrive.

And since we can't be everywhere we want to be, we are including all the suggestions we have about ways to find treatment providers across the country who may be helpful to you and/or your partner.

To learn more about CRAFT, you can view a video about CRAFT that is a very informative overview here: ***http://bit.ly/HBO-CRAFT***.

CMC is such a big believer in the transformational power of family involvement that we wrote a book specifically for you! *Beyond Addiction: How Science and Kindness Help People Change* is co-authored by our Co-Founders Drs. Foote and Wilkens and the Director of our Family Services, Dr. Nicole Kosanke. It is a huge resource full of the latest information science has given us about how the use of substances affects the brain/body, reward/memory systems, and motivation and learning. It is also a thorough description of the principles of Community Reinforcement and Family Training (CRAFT) which are some of the skills in the 20 Minute Guide as well. The book also contains very clear suggestions about ways you can think about your participation in the change process moving forward. We hope that you consider reading it as a way to enhance your thinking about behavior change. ***http://amzn.to/1mDMSA0***

You may want to consider attending one of our CRAFT classes. These classes are another user-friendly way to be exposed to the skills of CRAFT either in person or in the comfort of your own home. Visit our website for more information: ***http://motivationandchange.com/craftclass/***

CMC partnered with Bountiful Films and Magnify Digital on a first-of-its-kind online resource based on the 20 Minute Guide, CRAFT and motivational strategies. **Addiction. The Next Step** *(http://addictionthenextstep.com/)* is a website and an Interactive Guide *(http://addictionthenextstep.com/interactive-guide/)* built with financial support from the Telus Fund. The Interactive Guide enables visitors to define their own journey through videos, tips, and other tools designed to teach concerned family members how to communicate in a manner that *motivates their loved one toward change, while reducing family fear and stress.* The Interactive Guide offers a range of scenarios that represent the issues families face when dealing with a substance use problem. Drs. Jeff Foote and Carrie Wilkens, co-founders of the Center for Motivation and Change, deliver advice and practical tools to support your efforts toward changing the dynamics of your home and family.

Finally, we would like to extend an invitation to join our newsletter which we hope will become a welcomed entry into your inbox once a month. It will be loaded with helpful information about how to achieve and maintain your goals (and those of your loved one), wellness tips (recipes, exercise, self-care), current research in the field, CRAFT tips, ways to keep your motivation engaged, and more (some fun stuff will be woven in as well!). Our hope is that it inspires you and provides a monthly dose of support and interesting information. ***http://bit.ly/cmcnewsletter***

If you fill out this form, the newsletter will come to your email once a month.

ADDITIONAL CRAFT RESOURCES

Dr. Robert Meyers (Bob) is the father of the CRAFT approach and he has created several ways your can find CRAFT support:

WEBSITE: The website has a list of certified CRAFT providers.
http://www.robertjmeyersphd.com/craft

BOOK: *Get Your Loved One Sober: Alternatives to Nagging, Pleading, and Threatening*, by Dr Robert Meyers and Brenda Wolfe. *http://amzn.to/1mDN5TJ*

ONLINE: Recently, Bob teamed up with Cadence Online to launch Parent CRAFT, an online training for parents concerned about changing drug and alcohol behaviors in their children. The innovative online program takes the empirically-studied behavioral science of CRAFT and brings it to life in a highly engaging, interactive film-based course. They bring to life exercises that teach parents to understand their child's substance use pattern, improve their communication skills, develop methods of behavior management and learn when and how to guide them to accept professional help. We recommend that you go to *https://www.cadenceonline.com/* as these videos are a great way to access CRAFT strategies no matter where you live.

The Partnership at Drugfree.org has ever-evolving resources available, including a helpline just for family members seeking help for themselves or a loved one struggling with substance abuse. The Partnership hotline is staffed by well-trained professionals. They can also refer parents for peer-to-peer coaching with parents trained in the 20 Minute Guide system of support and we can fully vouch for these parent coaches...they are awesome, committed and well-trained individuals who can offer you a lot! 1-855-DRUGFREE or 855-378-4373. *http://www.drugfree.org/*

We are great advocates of evidence-based treatments like CBT, MI, and CRAFT and the more you can be vocal about your desire for these services to be available in your area, the more we can influence greater change in the field of addiction treatment so that family members and patients alike have more options individualized to meet their needs.